ENGLISH **PANO**

A course for adv

STUDENT'S BOOK

Felicity O'Dell

CAMBRIDGE
UNIVERSITY PRESS

PUBLISHED BY THE PRESS SYNDICATE OF THE UNIVERSITY OF CAMBRIDGE
The Pitt Building, Trumpington Street, Cambridge CB2 1RP, United Kingdom

CAMBRIDGE UNIVERSITY PRESS
The Edinburgh Building, Cambridge CB2 2RU, United Kingdom
40 West 20th Street, New York, NY 10011–4211, USA
10 Stamford Road, Oakleigh, Melbourne 3166, Australia

First published 1998

Printed in the United Kingdom at the University Press, Cambridge

ISBN 0 521 47690 9 Student's Book
ISBN 0 521 47691 7 Teacher's Book
ISBN 0 521 47692 5 Set of 2 cassettes

Contents

Unit		Reading/listening	Speaking/writing
1	Launched into space	Listening – Interviews	Writing – An article based on an interview
2	Spreads straight from the fridge	Reading – Slogans	Speaking – Sounds of English; agreeing
3	Rhymes and rhythms	Listening – Songs	Speaking – Rhymes and rhythms
4	Read all about it!	Reading – Editorials	Writing – Presenting a point of view
5	Playing games	Listening – Word games	Speaking – An informal way of asking questions
6	The IT revolution	Reading – Computer information	Writing – Being brief and to the point
7	From another world	Listening – Travel accounts	Speaking – Making a presentation
8	Gather ye rosebuds	Listening – Poems	Writing – Poems
9	Where do you get your energy?	Listening – Current affairs	Speaking – Making a current affairs programme
10	The perfect pair	Reading – Short story	Writing – Narrative
11	The enemy is complacency	Listening – Public speeches	Speaking – Rhetorical devices
12	An excellent first half	Reading – Business report	Writing – Report writing
13	On the brain	Listening – Lecture	Writing and speaking – Expanding notes
14	Laying down the law	Reading – Law report	Speaking – Difficult words to pronounce
15	Dramatic moments	Listening – Drama	Speaking – Expressing emotion; preparing a mini-drama
16	Tiny tot arrested	Reading – News articles	Writing – Punctuation
17	Have you heard the one about …?	Listening – Jokes	Speaking – Telling jokes
18	Potato-ology	Reading – Academic text	Speaking – Pronunciation of numbers
19	Business class	Listening – Business advice	Speaking – Speaking at meetings
20	Pocket money	Reading – Humorous writing	Writing – Article for class magazine
21	A compelling read	Reading – Blurbs	Writing – Presenting characters
22	Variety is the spice of life	Listening – Varieties of English	Speaking – Regional styles of speech; speaking in various styles

Grammar	Vocabulary	Study skills
Tense revision	Word groups	Keeping a record of your work
Transitive and intransitive verbs	Word forks	Choosing a grammar reference book
Articles	Colloquial language	Using dictionaries
Modality	Degrees of formality	Choosing a newspaper to read
Asking questions	Word formation	Coping with difficult listening texts
Present forms	Language of e-mail	Universal vocabulary exercises
Noun phrases	Affixes	
Grammar in poetry	Talking about poetry and the arts	Giving opinions about the arts
Degrees of formality in spoken English	Collocations	Some more universal vocabulary exercises
Tenses in narrative	Clichés	
Unreal past	Idioms and their origins	Speaking with a tape
Conjunctions and other linking words	Building business vocabulary	Revising your work
-ing forms	Vocabulary of lectures	Taking notes
Relative clauses	Commonly confused words	Summarising
Features of spoken grammar	Colours and their associations	
Prepositions	Newspaper language	Skimming and scanning
Word order	Puns	
Complex sentences in academic texts	Formal linking words and expressions	Putting it in your own words
Emphasis	Language of meetings	Guessing meaning from context
Gerunds and infinitives	Homographs	
Prepositions	Language of publicity	Suggestions for further reading
Flexible parts of speech	Varieties of vocabulary; US and British vocabulary	Assessing your own progress

Launched into space
Interviews

The main aspects of language worked on in this unit are:	• interviewing, being interviewed and listening to interviews • writing up an interview • tense revision • word groups • keeping a record of your work

Warm-up: Interviewing and being interviewed

You are going to interview someone in your class. An important part of doing a good interview is to ask interesting questions.

1 Look at the questions below. Do you think they are likely to lead to interesting answers? Why/Why not?

a How old were you when you started school?

b What is your most vivid memory of school?

c Do you like going to the dentist?

d What sorts of things frighten you?

e Have you ever broken the law?

f What do you consider as your greatest achievement(s) so far?

2 Work with a partner on the task below.

1 Write down another three interesting questions.
2 Compare your questions with those prepared by another pair of students.
3 Choose the question you like best from those prepared by the other pair.
4 Write the best questions selected on the board so that there is one question from each pair on the board.

3 Work in pairs, taking it in turns to interview and be interviewed. The interviewee should answer the interviewer's questions fully and should lead the interview in directions likely to interest the interviewer.

1 Interview your partner using some of the questions from the board. You will want to add other questions as the interview develops.
2 Make brief notes on your interviewee's answers.
3 Introduce the person to the class, describing two or three of the most interesting things you learnt about your partner during the interview.

Listening: Helen Sharman, Britain's first astronaut

1 🔊 Listen to the first part of an interview with Helen Sharman and complete the notes below.

By chance Helen Sharman heard an advert on the radio for
(1) ....
The offer was made by (2) .... to
somebody from (3) ....
Helen Sharman studied (4) .... at
university.
She had worked as (5) .... and
(6) ....
Applicants had to be:
(7) ....
(8) ....
The sports Helen Sharman liked were:
(9) ....
(10) ....
(11) ....
In her physical training programme she had to
(12) ....
There were (13) .... applicants for the job.

2 🔊 Now listen to the second part of the interview and answer these questions.

a Why are emergency rockets switched on before the actual launch?
b What was Helen doing when the launch took place?
c What does she mention seeing from space?
d What kinds of experiments does she mention doing?

3 🔊 Now listen to the last part of the interview and take notes on what you hear.

Born in Sheffield 1963.
First job with GEC in
London. Applied to be
astronaut 1989.
Learnt Russian.
Went into space 1991.

Vocabulary: Word groups

Learning theorists claim that grouping together words and expressions which you want to learn helps you to remember them. There are many different ways of grouping words and these exercises practise some of them.

1 A common way to group words is by topic. The interview is largely connected with the theme of space travel. Follow these instructions.

1 Take an empty page and write down any words and expressions from the tapescript on page 166 which are specifically concerned with this topic.
2 Can you think of five other words and expressions related to the theme? Write them down on the same page.
3 Compare the words and expressions you thought of with those noted by other students in the class. Add to your page any further useful words and expressions connected with space travel.

2 Words and expressions can also be grouped because they have some element in common. For example, you might choose to learn *absent-minded* and *to speak your mind* and *to put someone's mind at rest* together with *to be in two minds* or *blood-red, pillar-box red* and *cherry red* together with *brick-red*.

Here are some words and expressions from the listening text. Find at least two other words or expressions that you could group with each of them.

a weightlessness c build-up e to be in touch with
b safety d to take account of

3 You can also group words because they have some grammatical connection. For example, work out the grammatical connection between the words in each group and then add three more items to each group. The words you add do not need to come from the listening text.

a to drive, to find
b the Netherlands, the United Kingdom
c to pull out, to pull away
d space / a space; light / a light
e a desert / to desert; a record / to record

4 Another way of grouping words is by collecting different parts of speech from the same family i.e. words that share the same root. Complete the word family table on the left. The first row has been done for you as an example. Note that there will sometimes be more than one word in each box – and sometimes it is not possible to fill all the boxes.

Noun	Verb	Adjective	Adverb
advert(isement), advertiser, advertising	to advertise	advertised, advertising	—
		necessary	
experiment			
	to analyse		
science			
muscles			
		dangerous	
measurements			

Grammar: Verb revision

1 Here are some sentences from an article based on an interview with a film star. Look at the tenses used and answer the questions.

a When she was a child she used to spend hours just sitting by the river watching the fish.
  i What do the words *used to spend* convey?
  ii What other verb form could convey this idea in this context?
  iii Can this verb form suggested in (ii) always replace *used to*?

b She was going to get married that summer …
  i What do you think the next word will be? Why?
  ii What word could replace *going* in the example above?
c As a teenager she always used to boast, 'I'm going to move to Hollywood when I'm twenty-one.'
  i What might surprise a non-native speaker about the tense in the second part of what the teenager says?

ii This verb form is often found after the time conjunction *when*. Name six other conjunctions which could replace *when* in this sentence (without requiring the verb form *I'm* to change).

d When she was fifteen a new cinema was being built a stone's throw from her home.

  i What difference would it make to the meaning if the verb form was *was built* rather than *was being built*?

  ii What difference would it make to the meaning if the verb form was *had been built* rather than *was being built*?

e Looking to her future she claims that she will have retired by the time she is forty.
How old will she be when she retires?

2 Part of working with verb forms is thinking about tenses. However, another part involves thinking about whether a gerund or an infinitive is necessary.

Answer the questions. Begin your answer with a gerund or an infinitive as required.

Example: What are your plans for Saturday evening?
To go to the ice rink.

a What are your plans for Saturday evening?
b What do you often dream about?
c When you were small, what did your parents use to threaten to do if you were naughty?
d Why do you want to improve your English?
e What is your greatest ambition?
f What do you consider your greatest success?
g What do you have most difficulty with in English?
h What do you feel passionately about?

3 Here are some sentences from an interview with the American film star, Robin Williams. Put the verbs in brackets into the appropriate forms.

a *Jumanji* – its awkward title .... (not prevent) it .... (take) $90 million in America in the last two months – .... (be) a kids' film that .... (not respect) boundaries. I ask *Jumanji*'s star, Robin Williams, who .... (briefly confine) to a hotel room, if this interpretation .... (ring) any bells with him. The hyper-alternative comic .... (turn) mainstream film star, whose improvisational brilliance .... (harness)

.... (give) voice to a Disney genie in *Aladdin*, ... (see) the point instantly.

b From an only averagely dysfunctional home near Detroit, the young Williams .... (dress) in a blazer and .... (send) to what he .... (call) a Dead Poets' Society school. There he .... (pick on) for being short.

c When he .... (be) 16, his family .... (uproot) to California and Williams .... (feel) he was home at last. All along, during the formality and isolation of his childhood, he .... (create) a hysterical, imaginative domain of his own, ... (make) his toys speak, ... (manoeuvre) large armies across carpets. 'You know,' he .... (say), 'I .... (not have) far .... (look) for my inner child.'

d Success and failure both .... (hit) Williams hard. While his popular sitcom character Mork .... (charm) America, Williams .... (lead) a wild private life. One ex-girlfriend claimed he .... (threaten) .... (jump) out of a window if she .... (leave) him. Williams .... (not recall) this and .... (suspect) it .... (be) a basement window. But he .... (remember) a director at this time .... (threaten) .... (sack) him from the film if he .... (arrive) once more on set with a hangover.

Writing: Writing up an interview

Magazine interviews with famous people do not usually simply say things like *I asked if he enjoyed school and he said that he didn't*. They use a variety of techniques and include extra information to make the article more vivid and interesting for the readers.

1 Work with a partner. Follow these instructions.

1 Read the following ideas for making an article based on an interview more interesting.
   - Describe the person's appearance.
   - Comment on the interviewee's voice.
   - Describe what the person is doing at the time of the interview.
   - Compare the person to someone else.
   - Quote the person directly.
   - Give your own personal opinion of the interviewee.
   - Include points about the interviewee which may surprise the reader.
   - Use unusual and interesting vocabulary.
   - Vary sentence length.
   - Include extra information about the interviewee (e.g. in brackets or between dashes or commas).
   - Vary tense and sentence structure.
   - Occasionally use the present simple tense to convey an idea of immediacy.

2 Look at each of the four extracts in *Grammar* Exercise 3. Can you find examples of any of the points listed above? How could any of the points listed above but not exemplified in the extracts have been included?

3 Can you think of any other different ways for making a magazine article based on an interview more interesting for the readers?

2 Using as many of the ideas from Exercise 1 as possible, write up either the interview with Helen Sharman or your interview with your partner at the beginning of the unit.

Study skills: Keeping a record of your work

It can be difficult for advanced students to assess their progress. Why do you think this is the case?

A good way of observing your progress can be to keep a record of your work. This will not only help you to see what you have done but will also remind you of your previous level. Here are three exercises which will help you to keep a record of your level of English now.

1 The following kind of test is said to be a particularly good indicator of someone's level of English. Fill in each of the blanks with one word only.

The text is an extract from an interview with Bret Ellis, one of the new generation of American writers, author of *American Psycho*, *The Rules of Attraction* and *The Informers*.

He was hailed as a literary brat at 21 and, with *American Psycho*, damned as a misogynist madman at 27. Bret Easton Ellis lives in Manhattan's East Village, the stylish and sinister triangle (1) .... aggressive chic meets druggy grunge. (2) .... up his street, I feel I've wandered into (3) .... of his listless, threatening fictions. On the wall facing his apartment block (4) .... has written 'Insomnia looms' in blue chalk. Ellis is whey-faced and dressed (5) .... black ('I have a sense of propriety about interviews,' he says). I am (6) .... immediately by (7) .... boyish he looks – and will always look – with his

jowly cheeks, doleful brown (8) ...., turned-down
mouth and dimpled chin. He has long ears, hairy hands and a
(9) .... spots between his triangular eyebrows.
(10) .... is the face of a ruined choirboy.

His large, one-room, second-(11) .... apartment is
like the apartment of one of the more horrifying
(12) .... in *The Informers*, his latest book: empty. He has
lived there for seven years, (13) .... since he came to
New York, but it has the melancholy air of an apartment that has
never (14) .... properly moved into. It is often
(15) .... that you know a man by his bathroom. It's
clean and white and bare with bottles of vitamins,
(16) .... blades, tissues and a toothbrush on a glass shelf.

Ellis (17) .... born in Los Angeles where he lived for
18 years. He has always been close (18) .... his mother
and two sisters but his father – (19) .... well-off real
estate analyst – was 'violent, emotionally abusive, very difficult to
live with'. He wipes his hand across (20) .... face.

2 Note down in the box the score out of 20 which you got in this test. Also make a note of any special language areas which your teacher says you could usefully do extra work on.

> Score:
>
> Specific language areas to work on:

3 Work with a partner, but not with the person you interviewed at the beginning of the unit. Interview each other, recording your interviews.

Use these questions when you interview each other. They should help you to make appropriate plans for your programme of studies over the next few months.

a Why do you want to learn English?
b What have you particularly enjoyed and what have you not liked about learning English in the past?
c In what ways do you think you are most likely to use English in the future?
d How well equipped do you feel you already are to use English in these situations?
e How do you plan to work on your English over the next year – apart from coming to class?
f What do you feel you particularly need to work on in your English studies over the next few months?

Add at least two more questions of your own choice to ask your partner.

Keep a copy of your recording and write the date on it. When you have finished working with this book, listen again to your recording. However good your English may be now, you should notice by the end of the course that you can speak more fluently, more accurately and with a greater range of expression than you did when you made this recording.

4 Write a composition for your teacher entitled either *The Pleasures and Problems of Learning English* or *A Memorable English Lesson*.

Ask your teacher to correct it, drawing attention to all your mistakes and commenting not only on accuracy but also on the content and organisation of your composition and the range of vocabulary and structures you use.

Keep your essay and the comments on it so that you can refer to it later in the course.

The main aspects of language worked on in this unit are:	• slogans • English sounds • transitive and intransitive verbs • agreeing • word forks • choosing a grammar reference book

---

Warm-up: Catchy phrases

1 Discuss the following with a partner.

a What is
  – a proverb?
  – a slogan?
  – graffiti?
b What is the purpose of each of them?
c Do they have anything in common?

2 Look at the collage. Find six examples of proverbs, six slogans and six pieces of graffiti.

Can you think of two more proverbs, slogans and pieces of graffiti (in English, if possible)?

Reading: Slogans

1 Read the following extract from the *Cambridge Encyclopedia of the English Language* and answer these questions.

a How did the word *slogan* originate? Has the word come a long way from its original meaning?
b What does the extract suggest that slogans, proverbs and graffiti have in common?

2 Discuss with a partner.

a Which of the examples illustrated are not concerned with selling commercial products?
b Which do you think is the best example of each of the five different points made about the structure of slogans?
c Look at the collage on page 12. Which of the points made in the text about the structure of slogans (and proverbs and graffiti) are illustrated by each of the examples in the collage?

3 Here are some more examples of well-known slogans. Match the slogan on the left with the type of product advertised on the right.

a Spreads straight from the fridge	cream cakes
b Top people read *The Times*	credit card
c We're getting there	army
d Persil washes whiter	shampoo
e Your country needs you	newspaper
f Naughty but nice	washing powder
g Just wash 'n' go	margarine
h Your flexible friend	railway service

4 Which of the points made in the extract about the structure of slogans do the examples in Exercise 3 illustrate?

5 If possible, find some further examples of slogans illustrating each of the points made in the article in an English language magazine.

Britain's most sought after assortments.

Simply beautiful. And beautifully simple.

THE DIFFERENCE IS DEBENHAMS

If it's delicious and light, it's Delight

Originally the word *slogan* was used to describe the battle-cry or rallying-cry of a Scottish clan. Today the application is different but the intention behind modern slogans is much the same – to form a forceful, catchy, mind-grabbing utterance which will rally people, in this case to buy something, or to behave in a certain way. Indeed the force of the hard sell with which some slogans are placed before the public would no doubt have received the enthusiastic approval of any ancient Highlander.

In their linguistic structure, slogans are very like proverbs (or graffiti). Sentences tend to be short with a strong rhythm:
- Safety First.
- Beanz Meanz Heinz
- Ban the Bomb
- Walls Have Ears

They often have a balanced structure, especially if they get at all lengthy:
- Make love, not war.
- When you need Aspirin, drink Disprin.

There can be striking use of figurative language:
- Terylene keeps its promises
- Switch on the Sunshine (Kellogg's cereals)

Frequent use is made of alliteration and rhyme:
- Guinness is good for you
- Electrolux brings luxury to life
- Drinka pinta milka day
- Put a tiger in your tank (Esso petrol)
- You'll wonder where the yellow went
  When you brush your teeth with Pepsodent.

And several mimic a conversational style:
- It's fingerlickin' good (Kentucky Fried Chicken)
- I bet (s)he drinks Carling Black Label
- That'll do nicely (American Express)

As these examples suggest, slogans are used for far more than advertising commercial products, but are an essential part of all campaigns – political, safety, protest, health, environmental and so on. Indeed, one of the first steps in any campaign is to think up a good slogan, and some companies run regular competitions to obtain fresh ideas from the public. Invent a successful slogan today and (who knows?) you could be a millionaire tomorrow.

Grammar: Transitive and intransitive verbs

1 The title of this unit is *Spreads straight from the fridge*. Like a number of verbs in English, *spread* can be used either transitively or intransitively.

What is the difference between a transitive and an intransitive verb?

Here are some more examples of verbs which can be either transitive or intransitive. Are the examples correct or not? If not, correct them. If necessary check your answers in a grammar reference book or a dictionary.

a Can I borrow?
b Do you smoke cigarettes?
c The town is spreading rapidly.
d The toddler can already dress.
e She spread the map out on the table and started studying it.
f I haven't seen my parents for months and I miss terribly.
g This new strain of flu is spreading like fire.
h She spread herself out on the sofa.

2 In pairs, write sentences using each of these verbs (a) transitively and (b) intransitively.

Example: *'You can use my washing-machine on Mondays if you like,' the landlady added as an afterthought.*
He foolishly added his signature to the letter without reading it.

| add | blow | change | fit | miss | propose |
| run | shoot | spread | touch | turn | win |

Compare your sentences with those written by other pairs.

3 Is the object obvious in each of these sentences? What is it? Give the object for both verbs in *g*.

a I always find it very difficult to park in a small space.
b He has started drinking too much.
c How much did you spend at the supermarket today?
d They waved until the car had disappeared into the distance.
e Jill sings with great emotion.
f Jack is only four but he can already read.
g Bob washed and dressed.
h Mary rode very well although it was her first attempt.

4 With a partner add a different, less predictable object to each of the sentences in Exercise 3.

Example: *I always find it very difficult to park my lorry in a small space.*

Which pair thought of the most original object in each case?

Study skills: Choosing a grammar reference book

There are a lot of different grammar books for foreign learners of English which will help you to strengthen and develop your knowledge.

Work in pairs or groups of three. Follow these instructions.

1 Select the grammar book that you are considering using. If possible, have a range of grammar books in the class with different students following steps 2–5 with different books.
2 Choose either:
   a something in grammar that the class has been discussing recently (for example, the use of the past conditional tense – with no *if* clause – at the end of the first paragraph of the slogans text)
   b a grammar point that you have always found difficult
   c one of these typical problems – *make* and *do*; constructions with *wish*; causative *have/get*
3 Find the relevant explanation of the topic you selected and the accompanying exercises, if there are any, in the grammar book of your choice. Read the explanation and do the exercises.

4 Now answer all of the following questions which are relevant to the grammar book you were working with.
   a How easy was it to find the explanation and the exercises you wanted?
   b How clear was the explanation?
   c Did the explanation address the aspects of the problem that are difficult for you?
   d Were the exercises at the right level for you?
   e Was the answer key clear?
   f Did you get the answers correct?
   g Would you like to use the book again? Why/Why not?
5 Make a report to the class on the book you have been working with.
6 If other pairs or groups in the class have been working with the same grammar book, did they come to the same conclusion?

Speaking: Sounds of English

Unfortunately the sounds of English are not as closely linked to spelling as they are in some other languages. Work through the exercises below with a partner.

1 What comments can you make on the pronunciation of the following words? How can you check that your pronunciation is correct?

> sword   debt   could   height   weight
> plough   rough   cough

Look them up in a dictionary and note the phonetic transcription. The International Phonemic Alphabet or IPA is used by good dictionaries and other language reference books and it is printed at the back of this book for reference.

2 Read through the text about slogans on page 13 again. Underline any words which you think might cause difficulties for foreign learners of English. Check two of these in your dictionary and note down how they are written in the IPA.

3 Translate these words from the IPA into normal English spelling.

> njuːmætɪk   saɪkəʊ θerəpi   sæmən   trɒf
> dəʊ

Speaking: Agreeing

1 ▭ Listen to two people discussing some slogans. Answer these questions.

a Which slogans are they discussing?
b What do they think of them?
c What language do they use to show that they agree with each other?

British Rail – we're getting there!

2 You are going to agree with each other in the same way. In other words, you are going to be completing dialogues similar to the following example:

Example: *It's very cold today.*
          Yes, it is, isn't it? It's freezing.

First think of words (or expressions) that you might use to agree with these adjectives.

Example: cold   *freezing*

a hungry
b hot
c good (food)
d good (weather)
e good (film)
f nice (person)
g nice (party)
h tired
i hard (exam)
j pleased
k afraid
l worried

3 ▭ Now listen to the tape and agree with the speaker. Note that the tape does not go through the adjectives in Exercise 2 in the same order. Also some extra ones have been added at the end. Note also that the form of the prompt sentence varies a little – answer in any natural way.

4 ▭ Listen to the tape and answer the speaker in the affirmative. This time use alternative verbs in your answer. The first question in the exercise is given below with a suggested answer.

Example: *Did you like your first teacher at primary school?*
          Yes, I did. I adored her.

Vocabulary: Word forks

1 Look at part of the entry for *spread* from the *Cambridge International Dictionary of English*.

Find the right word to fill the gaps.

a Going to university has really allowed her to spread her
....

b We're meeting at lunchtime on Friday to give Anne her birthday present. Can you spread the ....?

c Jane lay spread-........................ on the grass in the sunshine, pretending to read.

d The survey found a .... spread of opinion on the issue of EEC regulations.

e Sue .... on a fantastic spread after the meeting.

f The local newspaper published a double-........................ spread about the pop group's visit to the town.

A word fork is a fork-shaped diagram like those below. A word fork helps you to write down three or more collocations (or words that frequently occur together) based on one word. Here are some examples, associated with the word *reference*.

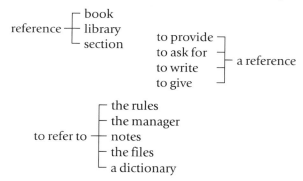

2 Choose one of the expressions from the *reference* word forks to complete these sentences.

a There is a handy .... at the back of the dictionary with lists, for example, of irregular verbs and common abbreviations.

b The speaker talked for half an hour without hesitation and without once ....

c As the head of a university department, a professor often has to .... for former students.

d If you have a problem with the service in this shop, please ....

e A good grammar and dictionary are essential .... for language students.

---

with leaves and flowers on it ● *a spray of chrysanthemums*

spread (obj) /spred/ v past **spread** to (cause to) cover, reach or have an effect on a wider or increasing area ● *The fire spread very rapidly because of the strong wind.* [I] ● *It started off as cancer of the liver but it spread to other areas of the body.* [I] ● *The redundancies are spread across the clothing, banking and building industries.* [T] ● *We spread the picnic rug out on the ground and sat down to eat.* [T] ● *The AIDS virus is spread* (=given to other people) *through contact with blood and other body fluids.* [T] ● *For this exercise you need to spread your arms out above your head.* [T] ● *She spread her toast with a thick layer of butter./She spread a thick layer of butter on her toast.* [T] ● *It's a special sort of butter that spreads easily even when cold.* [I] ● *The suburbs spread out for miles to either side of the city.* [I] ● *Slowly a smile spread across her face.* [I] ● *The votes were fairly evenly spread between the candidates.* [T] ● *Are you spreading* (=telling a lot of people) *gossip/rumours again?* [T] ● *She's got family spread (out) all over the world.* [T] ● *If we spread* (=share) *the work out between us it won't seem so bad.* [T] ● *If something is spread over a period it happens during that time, often in stages: I prefer to spread the cost of bills over a few months.* [T] ○ *The course is spread over two years.* [T] ○ *The repayments on the loan can be spread out over three years.* [T] ● *If something spreads like wildfire, it spreads extremely quickly: As soon as one child has contracted the disease it spreads like wildfire throughout the school.* [I] ● *If you spread your wings you use your abilities for the first time in your life to do new and exciting things: She'd been working for the same company for fifteen years and it was time to spread her wings.* ● *To spread the word is to communicate a message to a lot of people: A lot of companies regard television advertising as the most effective way of spreading the word.* ○ *We've arranged a meeting for next Thursday so if you see anyone do spread the word.* ● *If someone is spread-eagled they are lying with their arms and legs stretched out: She was lying spread-eagled on the grass.*

spread /spred/ n ● *The spread of AIDS in the last few years has been alarming.* [U] ● *The spread of something is the area or range covered by it: The survey found a wide spread of opinion over the proposed new building.* [U] ● In a newspaper or magazine, a spread is a large article or advertisement covering one or more pages: *There's a double-page spread on the latest fashions.* [C] ● A spread is a soft food for putting on bread and biscuits: *cheese/chocolate/fish spread* [U] ○ *There's bread and various spreads for tea.* [C] ● Spread is also *Am for* RANCH (=a large farm on which cattle and horses are kept). [C] ● *(Br and Aus dated)* A spread is also a meal, esp. one for a special occasion with a lot of different dishes arranged on a table: *Sheila laid on/(Br also) put on* (=made) *a lovely spread for us.* [C]

spread-sheet /spred ʃiːt/ n [C] a computer program

3 Now with a partner complete some word forks of your own. Use a dictionary to help you if necessary. Follow these instructions.

1 Write down three adjectives which collocate with the noun *spread*.

2 Write down three nouns which collocate as objects with *spread* when it is used as a transitive verb.

3 Write down three nouns which collocate as subjects with *spread* when it is used as an intransitive verb.

Middle-aged spread

4 Work with a different partner. Look up the word which the teacher gives you in an English learner's dictionary and follow these instructions.

1 Write one or more word forks focusing on the most useful collocations which the dictionary suggests for that word.

2 Write a gap-filling exercise for other students like Exercise 1 on *spread*.

3 Exchange exercises with each other. Use your dictionaries to complete each other's sentences.

Rhymes and rhythms
Songs

The main aspects of language worked on in this unit are:	• learning from songs • rhymes and rhythms • articles • colloquial language • using dictionaries

Warm-up: Songs

Listen to the songs brought in by the teacher or students in the class. Discuss the following.

a Can you as a class understand most of the words?
b What is the basic message of the song?
c Do the words of the song rhyme? If so, give some examples of rhymes used.
d Do the words include any especially interesting or curious examples of language use?
e Do you like this song? Why/Why not?

Listening: An old and a new song

1 The first song is a well-known Scottish folk song about a hero called Bonnie Prince Charlie who claimed the crown of Britain. He lost to the English at the Battle of Culloden in 1746 and fled to the Isle of Skye, dressed as the maid of Flora Macdonald.

Before listening to the song, read the words and decide which
of the rhyming possibilities seems to fit best.

Speed bonny boat
Like a bird on the *ring/swing/wing*
'Onward' the sailors *fly/cry/try*
Carry the lad
who's born to be king
Over the sea to Skye

Wild the winds howl
Loud the waves *pour/roar/draw*
Thunderclaps rend the air
Baffled our foes
Stand on the *door/shore/floor*
Follow they will not *care/dare/bear*

Many's the lad
Fought on that *day/hay/fray*
Well the claymore did *shield/wield/field*
But when the night came
Silently lay
Dead on Culloden *shield/wield/field*

High the waves leap
Soft shall ye *creep/sleep/sweep*
Ocean's a royal bed
Rocked on the deep
Flora will *heap/keep/peep*
Watch o'er your weary head

⌨ Now listen to the song and check whether you chose the
correct words.

2 Now answer these questions.

a What is the basic mood of the song?
b Is it on the Scottish or the English side or is it neutral? How do
you know?
c How do you think this song would have been received in
London in 1746?

3 ⌨ Listen to the song again and sing it with the tape.

4 The second song is a modern one (1988), also
by a Scottish writer and singer.

⌨ Listen to the song and work out what its
main message is.

Are these statements true or false? Listen to
the song again if necessary.

a The singer trusts the government.
b The singer thinks that life is good now.
c The singer is an optimist.
d The singer is against European Union
regulations.
e The singer believes that more schools and
hospitals should be built.
f The singer approves of American military
support.
g The singer feels that we should do something
about the situation he is describing.

5 🔊 The words of the song are printed below but they are incomplete. Listen again and complete the words. Remember that the rhyme scheme can often help you to work out what the missing words might be.

It's hard times in the cities
And it's hard times ....
And the stockbrokers and bankers say that
things ....
The economy's on ....
And they've made a ....
That we'll feel the benefits in ....

Fifty years from now, maybe 50 years from now
We'll be ankle deep in ....,
Fifty years from now.
So stop that .... whining,
Look for the ....
Prosperity's around ....,
Fifty years from now
Now the government has done its best to bring
prosperity
And all its work is threatened by ....
If we're to be ....,
It just can't be ....
That .... is a luxury we simply can't
afford

Fifty years from now, maybe 50 years from now
It'll all be ....
Fifty years from now
In the meantime keep ....
And bear it ....
And do your starving ....
Or else they'll ....

Now the butter's piled ....,
We're producing far too much
But we can't afford to buy a bit to ....
And the seas are full of fish that the ....
But if they did the EEC would make them
....

Fifty years from now, maybe 50 years from now
Tell the gas board that ....
Fifty years from now
If you're old or on the dole
Then I know ....
By the thought that it'll ....
Fifty years from now
Now we can't go ....,
We need the cash for ....
Our generals and admirals must have
....
And schools don't ....
Like nuclear bombs and ....
That's why the country's overrun by
....

Fifty years from now, maybe 50 years from now
We'll be blackened heaps of cinders, 50 years
from now
If we ....
Without ....
There'll be nothing left ....
In 50 years from now

6 Discuss the political viewpoint of the singer with three or four other students. Think about these questions.

  a What are the main political points which are being made in this second song?
  b What do you think someone who had a different point of view to the singer might say to him about defence spending, EU fishing regulations and the US presence in Western Europe?
  c To what extent do you agree with the points being made in this song?

7 As a class, think about both of the songs which you have listened to. Answer these questions.

  a What is the connection between the two songs you have studied in this unit?
  b Can you think of any other songs which share this element – in any language? What are they and why were they written?
  c Do you think that songs are a good medium for messages of this kind? Why/Why not?

Speaking: Rhymes and rhythms

1 ⌨ Learning songs and poems which make effective use of both rhyme and rhythm can be an enjoyable way of improving your pronunciation. Follow these instructions.

1 Read the following poems aloud with the tape.
2 Comment on the use of rhyme and rhythm in each poem.
3 If you wish, learn one of the poems or one of the songs by heart.

Harrow-on-the-Hill

When melancholy Autumn comes to Wembley
And electric trains are lighted after tea
The poplars near the Stadium are trembly
With their tap and tap and whispering to me,
Like the sound of little breakers
Spreading out along the surf-line
When the estuary's filling
With the sea.

Then Harrow-on-the-Hill's a rocky island
And Harrow churchyard full of sailors' graves
And the constant click and kissing of the trolley buses hissing
Is the level to the Wealdstone turned to waves
And the rumble of the railway
Is the thunder of the rollers
As they gather up for plunging
Into caves.

There's a stormcloud to the westward over Kenton
There's a line of harbour lights at Perivale,
Is it rounding rough Pentire in a flood of sunset fire
The little fleet of trawlers under sail?
Can those boats be only roof tops
As they stream along the skyline
In a race for port and Padstow
With the gale?

The Flattered Flying-Fish

Said the Shark to the Flying-Fish over the phone:
'Will you join me tonight? I am dining alone.
Let me order a nice little dinner for two!
And come as you are, in your shimmering blue.'

Said the Flying-Fish 'Fancy remembering me,
And the dress that I wore at the Porpoises' tea!'
'How could I forget?' said the Shark in his guile:
'I expect you at eight!' and rang off with a smile.

She has powdered her nose; she has put on her things;
She is off with one flap of her luminous wings.
O little one, lovely, light-hearted and vain,
The Moon will not shine on your beauty again!

2 Bring to class an English song or poem which makes good use of rhyme and/or rhythm. Play it or read it to the class and explain what you find effective about the rhyme or the rhythm.

Vocabulary: Colloquial language

Colloquial language is language that is informal and used much more in conversation than in, say, formal writing. 'John's a nice bloke' is, for example, a colloquial way of saying 'John is a pleasant man.'

1 Can you find any examples of colloquial language in the second song you worked on in this unit? What would be the more formal equivalents of each of these colloquial words or expressions?

2 Some words have both an 'ordinary' and a colloquial meaning. For example, *kid* is a colloquial word for *child* or *to trick*, but its basic meaning is *a young goat*.

Do you know the colloquial meanings as well as the 'ordinary' ones of these words?

a bread	**f** jaw
b cool	**g** thick
c anorak	**h** wet
d jerk	**i** sack
e grub	**j** flash

3 Articles in popular music magazines are often written in an extremely colloquial style – they may use the language in such a creative and unusual way that they may be quite difficult to understand in places. The example of this style which you are going to read is about a band called The Make-Up, which was about to tour Britain.

Read the article and answer the questions below.

a What do you learn about the band The Make-Up from the article?

b How does the writer feel about their work?

c The writer uses some quite unusual images. What are they and how effective do you think they are?

Underline the strikingly colloquial words and expressions.

MAKE-UP CALL

Flash, distinctly flash, THE MAKE-UP are the current coolest band in America.

They're jamming James Brown through the punk rock mincer and coming up with sexy, sassy anthems.

They've cut four hard-to-grab seven-inch singles and an album. They combine idealism, rock 'n' roll and the funk with natty stage threads and an interview technique that makes the prime-time Manics look like shy nowt-to-say librarians.

The Make-Up are an unpinned grenade and they are coming this way in the spring. Currently the best undiscovered band out there. If you don't get this band, you're brain dead. It's that simple.

Grammar: Articles

1 Look at the passage about The Make-Up again. The sentences in this exercise come from the passage but the use of one of the articles is different. Is the sentence correct and meaningful? If so, how does the altered article affect the meaning?

a They're jamming James Brown through a punk rock mincer.

b They've cut four hard-to-grab seven-inch singles and the album.

c They combine idealism, rock 'n' roll and the funk with natty stage threads and the interview technique that makes the prime-time Manics look like shy nowt-to-say librarians.

d The Make-Up are the unpinned grenade and they are coming this way in the spring.

e The Make-Up are an unpinned grenade and they are coming this way in spring.

2 The pairs of sentences below differ only in their use of articles. What difference to meaning (or nuance) does this make?

1 a Sarah's studying at a music school in Leicester.
  b Sue's studying at the music school in Lancaster.
2 a Amanda's had a baby.
  b Annette's had the baby.
3 a Bill met a Japanese student on the train.
  b Ben met the Japanese student on a train.
4 a Suzanne wrote a most interesting composition.
  b Sylvia wrote the most interesting composition.
5 a A dog is a better companion than a cat.
  b The dog is a better companion than the cat.
6 a Tina stopped the car at the corner.
  b Betty stopped a car at the corner.
7 a Have you ever met the Member of Parliament?
  b Have you ever met a Member of Parliament?
8 a Jack entered college with three A-levels.
  b Jill entered the college to ask about courses.
9 a We first met at dinner.
  b We first met at the dinner.
10 a Michael Jones, the contemporary Welsh novelist, has also written a number of popular songs.
  b Michael Jones, a contemporary Welsh novelist, has also written a number of popular songs.
11 a An organisation has been set up to help the victims of crime.
  b An organisation has been set up to help the victims of the crime.
12 a Has he ever been in hospital?
  b Has he ever been in the hospital?

3 Fill in each of the blanks in the statements about articles below. You need only one word for each blank.

a *A* and *an* are called the .... article. *The* is called the .... article.

b You use .... or .... when you talk about a person or thing for the first time.

c You need to use the .... article when you are talking about someone's job, e.g. Margaret is .... physicist.

d You use *a* in front of words beginning with .... sounds and *an* in front of words beginning with .... sounds.

e *An* is used in front of a number of words beginning with 'h', e.g. ...., ... or ....

f You use *the* before a noun which has .... been mentioned before or of which there is only ....

g If you want to make a general statement about all things of a particular type, you can use the .... article with the singular form of a countable noun. (You can make a similar statement using the plural form of the noun but in that case you do .... use the article.)

h You do not use the article when you are making general statements using an .... noun.

i You can use *the* with some words, e.g. *rich*, ..., *young*, ... and *unemployed* in order to make general statements about all people of this type.

j You can use *the* with some nationality adjectives to refer to the people who live in a particular .... or to a group of people originating there.

k You can use the .... article with a singular count noun to refer to a system or service, e.g. *She doesn't like using .... telephone.*

l .... is sometimes used at the beginning of a noun group in which you refer to a well-known person's profession as well as their name, e.g. Leo Tolstoy, ... nineteenth-century Russian novelist.

4 Write example sentences to illustrate points b–l in Exercise 3.

5 Nouns or adjectives beginning with *u* may be preceded by *a* or by *an*. When is *a* used and when is *an* used?

Write *a* or *an* in front of each of these adjectives and then add an appropriate noun after each one. The first one has been done as an example.

a ubiquitous *phrase*
ugly
ulterior
ultimate
unanimous
uniformed
unique
universal

unilateral
unusable
unworthy
usable
useless
usual
unusual

Speaking: New words for an old song

You are going to write some new words for a song in English – keeping the original tune. Work in groups of three or four and follow these instructions.

1 Choose a song that everyone in the class knows well – perhaps one of the ones from this unit, or one that is currently popular or one from your own language.
2 You are going to write new words for the song. The song can be humorous or serious, as you prefer. The topic for your song should relate in some way to the experience shared by the students in your class – it could be about students or teachers in your school, it could be about an event that you have all been to recently, it could be about the region you are studying in.
3 Decide on the topic for the song and then work out what words would fit the rhythm of the song. Write down the words.
4 Practise singing them in your small group.
5 Organise a concert for the class where each group sings its song.

Study skills: Using dictionaries

One of the most important study skills for any language student is the ability to use dictionaries easily and effectively. Practise by doing these exercises. Use an English-English dictionary for foreign learners to work on Exercises 1 to 5 and a bilingual dictionary for Exercises 6 and 7.

1 A dictionary can tell you about meaning. All these words from the music magazine article have a number of distinct meanings. How many can you think of? Look them up in your English-English dictionary and write down any meanings you did not know in your vocabulary notebook in any appropriate way. For example, you could write them in a sentence or give a translation.

lean   mean   sound   course

2 A dictionary can tell you about grammar. Find the answers to these questions by looking at your dictionary.

a What are the past tense and the past participle forms of the verbs *strive* and *seek*?
b What are the plural forms of the nouns *syllabus* and *criterion*?
c What prepositions often follow the adjectives *dependent* and *independent*?

3 A dictionary can tell you about collocations. Look up the word *set* and complete the following word forks.

set as noun

a .... ⊢ set
....

set as verb

a .... ⊢ sets
....

set as adjective

a set ⊢ ....
....
....

to set ⊢ ....
....

4 A dictionary can tell you about spelling. How do you spell the following words?

ˈbaɪsɪkəl əkɒməˈdeɪʃən rɪˈsiːt ɪmˈbærəst ˈɒfərɪŋ prɪˈfɜːrɪŋ

5 A dictionary can tell you about pronunciation. Look up the words in the chart in the dictionary and write them down in the IPA. Remember to indicate where the stress is.

Word	In IPA
arpeggio	
archaic	
archangel	
archbishop	
archipelago	
archive	
archivist	

6 Now take the bilingual dictionary which you normally use and answer these questions.

a Does it also give you information about meaning?
b Does it also give you information about grammar?
c Does it also give you information about collocation?
d Does it also give you information about spelling?
e Does it also give you information about pronunciation?

7 Using your bilingual dictionary, look up the following English words. Write down the translation(s) offered. Then look up those translations in the other end of the dictionary and see which English words are offered as equivalents.

English word	Translation(s)	English translations of word(s) in previous column
lean (*adj*)		
key (*adj*)		
to strive		
to thrive		
archaic		

8 It is, of course, very important to consolidate what you have learnt. Write a paragraph on any subject you like – a short story, perhaps, or a description of your classroom (or a song!) – using as many as possible of the words you have worked with in Exercises 1 to 7.

Read all about it!
Editorials

The main aspects of language worked on in this unit are:	• reading editorials • writing – presenting a point of view • modality • degrees of formality • choosing a newspaper to read

---

Warm-up: Giving your opinion formally and informally

1 Work with a partner. How do you feel about these three subjects?

a Killing elephants to get ivory.
b National lotteries.
c Reading newspapers.

How would you express your opinion if you were talking to a group of close friends and if you were writing a composition for a teacher? Follow these instructions:

1 Write down one sentence that you might say and one that you might write in such circumstances.
2 Take it in turns to read out one of the sentences to the other students in the class. They must guess whether you were reading the 'talking to friends' sentence or the 'composition' sentence.
3 What clues help you to work out whether something is in a formal or an informal style?

Reading: Choosing a newspaper to read

If you are interested in the news and like to follow it in your own language, reading an English-language newspaper regularly can be a very useful habit.

- Firstly, you will already know the content of many of the stories that you read and so it will be easier to work out the meanings of unfamiliar words and expressions.
- Secondly, you will easily pick up a lot of vocabulary as many words and expressions relating to news stories are used repeatedly from one issue of the paper to the next.

There are quite large differences, however, between the content and approach of various newspapers and, if you have access to a range of English-language papers, it is important that you read one that suits you. It can also be interesting to see just how different two or more newspapers can be.

1 Choose two different British newspapers. If possible, select a 'quality' paper (e.g. *The Times, The Guardian, The Independent*) and a tabloid (e.g. *The Mirror, The Mail, The Express* or *The Sun*) and, if possible, select two papers published on the same date.

If it is difficult to get hold of British newspapers, you can do this exercise with any English-language newspapers which you may be able to find in your area. The US paper *The Herald Tribune* is available quite widely throughout the world and there may be other English-language papers published in your own country.

Complete this table for each of the papers you have chosen. Check that you understand all the vocabulary in the table before you start to complete it.

Name of paper:		
Number of pages:		
Price:		
What is the main story? Write down the headline and the topic.		
How many pages are devoted to each of these: foreign news? home news? sport? business? entertainment?		
Is there/Are there: any cartoons? any comic strips? a crossword? a horoscope?		
Are there any articles about: the Royal family? soap stars? violent crimes? film stars? your own country? If yes, note down the main focus of the story/stories.		
What are the editorials about? Note down the main point of each.		
Look at the job adverts (if there are any). What kinds of jobs are being advertised?		
Look at the letters page. What subjects are the letters concerned with?		
Do you think you would be interested in reading this newspaper again? Why/Why not?		

Reading: Editorials

1 An editorial is a newspaper article in which the editor gives his or her opinion on an item in the news. There is no pretence at factual reporting as there will be in most of the news stories in the paper.

Look quickly at the example of an editorial from *The Times* below and decide:

a what the topic is
b what the editor's opinion is.

"It's for putting umbrellas in."

Elephantine success

But continuing the total ban on the ivory trade is essential

The illegal international trade in wildlife and wildlife products is estimated by Interpol at $5 billion a year. The Convention on International Trade in Endangered Species of Flora or Fauna (CITES), to which more than 120 countries are party, bans or restricts international trade in some 34,000 endangered or rare species. Yet the loss of species in many regions is dramatic. Sanctions are weak and rarely invoked even against the most guilty countries. In the year to February 1994, British customs seized 12,853 items – endangered species or products made from them – at Heathrow, Gatwick and Stansted alone. Europe is the world's second largest market for wild birds, some of them on the danger list.

Public protest and the prestige of CITES are vital to improving this record. The single spectacular success CITES can point to is the total ban in the trade on elephant products, including ivory, introduced in 1989. 'Controlled' trade in ivory had been a dismal failure; in ten years, Africa's elephant population had fallen from 1.3 million to 600,000. Poachers have few incentives today. Although demand in Japan is still very high, the Western ivory market has collapsed and the price – contrary to predictions by opponents of the ban – has fallen from £90 a pound to less than £2. Now South Africa, which has always objected to the ban, wants the CITES meeting in Florida to relax it, permitting it to export elephant hides, prized for such items as elefoot wastepaper bins and Texan cowboy boots. It argues that it needs to cull the beasts, and could raise $500,000 for conservation that way – and that, if honoured, it will co-operate with the ban on ivory sales. Perhaps, but South African wardens are on record that they have millions-worth of tusks which they hope one day to sell. Conservationists, pointing to an upsurge in poaching in Zambia and Tanzania, believe that ivory traders would take a partial relaxation of the ban as a green light.

Britain is wavering but inclined to support South Africa. It should do no such thing. If South Africa is genuine about the ivory ban, let it first destroy its stockpiles. If it is short of money, let it charge its tourists more to visit its game parks. An elephant hide is worth $1,000. Kenya calculates that during its lifespan an elephant brings in $1 million in tourist revenue. In Africa, where governments are weak if not corrupt, the odds are against the elephant surviving even a partial resumption of trade in its carcass. That should be the sole consideration for CITES.

2 Now read the editorial more carefully and answer the following questions.

a What is CITES?
b What is the significance of the following sums of money in the editorial?
 – $5 billion
 – £90
 – £2
 – $500,000
 – $1,000
 – $1,000,000

c What is the significance of the following numbers in the editorial?
 – 120
 – 34,000
 – 12,853
 – 1.3 million
 – 600,000
d Why do you think the sub-editor of the newspaper chose this particular headline?

Grammar: Modality

Modality is the term used to refer to the ways in which we express ideas of possibility, obligation, willingness, advisability and so on. Very often modality is expressed by using modal verbs such as *must, could, will* and *should*. However, it can also be expressed in other ways, for example, by

- adverbs, e.g. *probably* or *ideally*
- adjectives, e.g. *essential* or *reluctant*
- nouns, e.g. *likelihood* or *certainty*
- phrases, e.g. *the chances are* or *to be on the cards*

1 Look at the editorial *Elephantine Success* again and find examples of modality expressed in ways other than by modal verbs, in the following places:

a one from the heading.
b one from the beginning of the second paragraph (line 20).
c one in the second half of the second paragraph (line 42).
d one from the third paragraph (line 59).

2 Rewrite the sentences with the modality expressions you noted down in the previous exercise. Use modal verbs instead of the original modality words or phrases.

3 🔊 Listen to the tape. Which expression of modality does the speaker use in each case? And what idea does the expression convey? The first one has been done for you.

	Expression	Idea
1	may perhaps	possibility
2		
3		
4		
5		
6		
7		
8		
9		
10		

4 What other expressions of modality can you think of to add to those you have been discussing above? Follow these instructions.

1 Write down as many as you can.
2 Exchange your list with a partner.
3 Write sentences about your own situation in school to illustrate the expressions of modality on your partner's piece of paper.
4 Show the sentences you wrote to each other. Have you each written correct examples? Ask your teacher if you are not sure.

Vocabulary: Degrees of formality

Editorials in papers like *The Times* are usually written in a very formal style. Those in *The Sun* are very different. They use their own very informal language, characteristic of the tabloid press.

1 Read the editorial from *The Sun*, printed on the day when Britain's first National Lottery was launched.

Highlight all the words in it that you would be unlikely to find in more formal writing.

YOU LUCKY LOTT

Life will never be the same again after this week ...

ESPECIALLY for the lucky punter who will become Britain's first National Lottery millionaire.

Forget the moaners who say it's just another tax dressed up as a game. Who ever got rich paying VAT?

The Lottery is going to be great fun. Every one of us will get a thrill by watching the numbers drawn on live TV.

Buy a ticket today. Don't forget ... it could happen to you.

2 Do you notice anything else apart from vocabulary that is typical of a tabloid newspaper style in the editorial from *The Sun*? Think about:

– sentence length
– punctuation
– layout
– content
– anything else that strikes you.

3 Now look back at the *Elephantine Success* editorial. Follow these instructions.

1 Underline any words and expressions in it that seem to be characteristic of a particularly formal style.
2 Compare the editorial from *The Times* with the one from *The Sun* from the point of view of sentence length, punctuation, layout, content and any other points you noticed about editorial style in *The Sun*.

4 Here are some other sentences from popular newspapers. Underline any characteristically tabloid words and expressions in them and write them in a more neutral way.

a A jailbird wangled a day's freedom yesterday to go fox-hunting with 50 posh pals of Prince Charles.
b We're giving away lashings of lolly this week to some of our particularly lucky readers.
c A man was fighting for life last night after being gunned down in a pub brawl.
d BT operator Jack Constable was roasted for spending two seconds too long in the loo.
e A man in a Birmingham street was knocked cold yesterday by a flying pooch.
f The coolest blokes dress like telly nerd Mr Bean, fashion experts claim.
g Leftie teachers have voted to wreck the government's plans for school tests for all seven-year-olds.
h Our readers agree that yobs must be barred from football stands.
i A popular TV star has finally dumped her hubbie after their latest bust-up.
j Sunny days are here again, folks, and cars loaded with kids, picnics and beach gear jammed all roads to the south coast yesterday.

5 If you can get a copy of a popular English-language newspaper, follow these instructions with a partner.

1 Take a page from a popular newspaper.
2 Find as many characteristically tabloid words and expressions as you can.
3 Write them down with their more formal equivalents.
4 Test other students in the class. Do they know what the tabloid words and expressions you found mean?

Writing: Presenting a point of view

1 As a class look at this list of useful phrases for giving opinions. Which preposition can follow each of the phrases? Finish each sentence in any appropriate way, relating your answers to one of the following topics – conservation of the environment, gambling or the power of the press.

a We totally disagree
b We have a firm belief
c We concur
d The answer depends
e We are in complete agreement
f Our attitude

g There is no reason
h There is little point
i Our opinion
j It reminds us
k In comparison
l In contrast

2 Work with a partner. You are going to write an article – the equivalent of an editorial – for a class magazine. Follow these instructions.

1 Choose your topic. You could write about:
 – something topical affecting the students in your college;
 – a controversial issue currently in the news;
 – a social issue you both feel strongly about.
2 Write three questions about your topic. The aim of the questions is to elicit opinions and ideas from other students on the subject you have selected, so make the questions as open and as stimulating as you can.
3 Work with a different person. Take it in turns to ask each other your questions. Answer the questions as fully as you can and continue discussing your chosen issues in any appropriate ways.
4 Note down the main points arising from the discussion of your own issue.
5 Rejoin your original partner and compare the answers which you each got. Do not start writing your editorial yet.

3 Follow these instructions with the partner you worked with in Exercise 2.

1 Decide on the main angle which your article is going to take. As in an editorial, the article should be presenting a strong opinion about the issue in question. You may, of course, choose to play devil's advocate, i.e. to provoke people by presenting a deliberately controversial point of view which is not your own.
2 Decide whether you are going to write in the style of a tabloid or a quality newspaper. A quality paper style will be easier for you as it is very much the style of a college composition whereas a tabloid style – although usually grammatically simple – is in a more distinct style, which you are unlikely to have had to write yourselves before. If you wish, one of you may write in tabloid style and one in quality newspaper style. Alternatively, you may work together in whichever style you prefer.
3 Write a plan for your article, using any of the ideas which came up in Exercise 2.
4 Write the article. Use at least some of the phrases from Exercise 1. Also try to use some of the expressions of modality which you worked on earlier in the unit.
5 Write a headline for your article.

4 Read the articles written by other pairs of students. Which articles are written in tabloid style and which in the style of quality papers?

If you read an article that you do not agree with, write a letter to the authors expressing your own opinion.

The main aspects of language worked on in this unit are:	• understanding and explaining games • coping with difficult listening texts • pronunciation – an informal way of asking questions • the grammar of questions • word formation

Warm-up: Language games

1 Discuss with a partner.

a What sort of games do you enjoy playing?
b Do you enjoy using games in lessons?
c What games have you used which provide helpful practice in learning English?
d Can you think of any other games which could be useful in English lessons? If so, describe them to your partner.

Listening: Word games

1 🎧 You are going to listen to an extract from a popular BBC radio panel game called 'Just a Minute'. Listen to the instructions explaining how the game is played.

Would it be possible to play this game in your class? If so, would the instructions need to be adapted at all?

2 🎧 The panellists on this radio programme are Clement Freud, Kenneth Williams, Derek Nimmo and Peter Jones. The subject that has to be talked about is 'what to do with the hole in a doughnut'. Read the dictionary definition of a doughnut and then follow the instructions below.

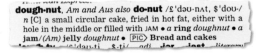

dough-nut, *Am and Aus also* **do-nut** /£ˈdəʊ·nʌt, $ˈdoʊ-/ *n* [C] a small circular cake, fried in hot fat, either with a hole in the middle or filled with JAM • *a* **ring** *doughnut* • *a* **jam**/(*Am*) **jelly** *doughnut* • PIC> **Bread and cakes**

1 Decide what sorts of things you think the panel may find to say about what to do with the hole in a doughnut.
2 Listen to the extract from the programme. What is in fact suggested?
3 Listen again and note down the challenges, why they were made and whether they were accepted or not.
4 Compare your notes with those taken by other students. Do your notes contradict each other at all?

3 🎧 Listen to the tape again and look at the tapescript on page 167 at the same time.

Correct or add to your notes if necessary.

Mark anything in the tapescript that you would like to ask about or comment on.

4 Note down some good topics for a game of 'Just a Minute' and play the game in your class.

5 Perhaps you found this listening extract quite difficult to listen to and understand. Think about the following questions.

a How difficult did you in fact find it?
b What made it difficult?
c Are there any other characteristics of listening texts that you are aware of that can make listening and understanding more difficult?
d Do you think you are likely to meet difficult characteristics of this sort in listening in real life?
e What can you do to help yourself cope with difficult listening of the sort you identified?

Speaking: An informal way of asking questions

1 🎧 Listen to some people playing a game where they have to guess what a story means. Notice how they ask questions.

2 🎧 Listen again and repeat the questions asked by the people in the dialogue.

Does the intonation used by the speaker in each question indicate any particular mood – surprise, amusement, frustration, interest, boredom, for example – or is the intonation used simply neutral?

3 🎧 Listen to the speakers on the tape and answer these questions.

a Are each of the utterances statements or questions?
b Does the intonation of each of the utterances convey any of the moods indicated in the previous exercise – or any other mood?

Now repeat each of the utterances after the speaker on the tape.

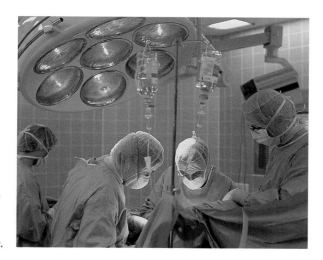

4 Read each of the sentences below either as a statement or as a question. The other students must recognise whether you asked a question or not and must make an appropriate response.

Notice that the response to the question will vary depending on where the speaker put the dominant stress in the question (e.g. it could equally well be on *Jane*, *Bill* or *well* in the first example).

a Janet knows Bill well.
b You played squash last night.
c The whole class passed the exam.
d Jack is going to Rome tomorrow.
e Elizabeth is planning to change her job soon.
f We were singing very loud.
g Jill is the person who you were telling me about last night.
h You wouldn't have agreed to play the game if you'd known what it involved.

5 Your teacher is going to tell you another puzzle story like the one you listened to in Exercise 1. Listen and ask questions. Try to use the kind of informal way of asking questions that we have been practising. Your teacher will only answer your questions if you get the intonation pattern correct.

Grammar: Asking questions

1 There are, of course, many situations in English when you will need to ask questions. Write down five questions that you think you would be likely to need in the following roles:

a As someone inquiring about the rules of a new game or sport.
b As a learner of English wanting to find out about aspects of the language.
c As a student who is interested in studying in an educational institution in an English-speaking country.
d As someone on the first day at work in an English-speaking environment.
e As a guest in an English-speaking hotel.

2 Look at the questions you wrote in Exercise 1 and follow these instructions.

1 Compare the questions which you wrote in Exercise 1 with those written by other students.
2 Work with another student and role play each of the following situations. Decide who is to be A and who is to be B. The student asking the questions should use as many as possible of the questions already discussed but may add any additional ones to fit the situations as they develop. The student answering the questions should use his or her imagination to answer in any way that might be appropriate.

a A is a learner of English and B is an English teacher who loves answering her students' questions.
b B has just arrived at the Buckingham Palace Hotel in London and A is a particularly helpful receptionist there.
c A is considering studying at a college in an English-speaking country. B is a student who has already been at that college for two years.
d B is on his or her first morning at work in a British workplace. A is someone who has worked there for a long time and has been told to help B get to grips with the new job. (First decide what kind of workplace you are in.)

3 Here is part of a dialogue about Loch Ness, a long and very deep lake in Scotland, famous for the legendary monster which is supposed to live there and which groups of scientists from Japan and elsewhere have occasionally tried to find – so far in vain.

What questions do you think are needed to complete the dialogue?

CHRIS: This is an interesting article.
JO:
CHRIS: It's about some scientific research they've been doing in Loch Ness.
JO:
CHRIS: No, not this time. They've been drilling into the bottom of the lake and bringing out cores which provide a record of how the climate and other things have changed over the last 10,000 years.
JO:
CHRIS: About six metres long. Apparently, they show that Scotland had a golden age about 2,000 to 4,000 years ago. The weather was amazingly different then.
JO:
CHRIS: The article says 'it basked in the same kind of climate that countries round the Mediterranean Sea enjoy today. Summers were hot, winters warmer and drier, the country was covered with lush green forests and there were clear blue skies for most of the year'. Sounds great. Wish it'd been like that when we were on holiday there!
JO:

CHRIS: It also talks about archaeological evidence which suggests that the population, which was rapidly growing during this balmy period, suddenly disappeared.

JO:

CHRIS: One theory is that the eruption of a volcano in Iceland might have caused cooling and crop failures. If that was the case, then they should find volcanic fragments in the cores.

JO:

CHRIS: Yes, they show the development of the Industrial Revolution through the increase and then decline of particles produced by coal and oil burning. The cores also record the peak in atmospheric nuclear testing – which was in 1963, apparently, – and, goodness me, they also reflect the nuclear accident at Chernobyl in 1986.

JO:

CHRIS: No, but with data as interesting as this, who needs monsters?

4 **Work with a partner and follow these instructions.**

1 Prepare another question and answer dialogue like the one in Exercise 3. The Chris and Jo dialogue was based on a newspaper article. You might like to base yours on a newspaper or magazine article. (The original article does not have to be in English if you do not have easy access to magazine or newspaper articles in English.)
2 First write your dialogue out in full.
3 Then write it out again with no questions, just the answers.
4 Exchange the incomplete dialogues with another pair and write in what you think the original questions were.
5 Compare your version with the original which the other pair wrote.

5 🔲 **Now listen to some people playing another game in which questions play an important role. Decide what the rules of the game they are playing are.**

Vocabulary: Word formation

1 **Look at these words which you have met in the unit so far and follow the instructions below.**

> deviation substance insert decorative atmospheric disappear

1 From these words, give three examples of a prefix.
2 What do each of these prefixes mean?
3 Give three examples of other words using each of these prefixes.
4 Give three examples of a suffix from the words above.
5 What do each of these suffixes mean?
6 Give three examples of other words using each of these suffixes.
7 What is the root of the word in each case?
8 Give an example of another word with each of these roots.

2 **Some affixes (prefixes and suffixes) have more than one meaning. What are the meanings of the underlined affixes in each case? Add an additional example of a word using the same affix with the same meaning, if possible – use your dictionary if necessary.**

a snow<u>bound</u> and north<u>bound</u>
b <u>anti</u>-vivisection and <u>anti</u>-coagulant
c hover<u>craft</u> and stage<u>craft</u>
d <u>cross</u>-channel and <u>cross</u>-cultural
e <u>well</u>-adjusted, <u>well</u>-documented and <u>well</u>-disposed
f news<u>worthy</u> and sea<u>worthy</u>
g <u>semi</u>-invalid and <u>semi</u>-circular
h editor<u>ship</u>, companion<u>ship</u> and statesman<u>ship</u>
i sudden<u>ly</u> and mother<u>ly</u>
j tonsill<u>itis</u> and football<u>itis</u>
k mono<u>gram</u> and milli<u>gram</u>
l <u>fore</u>arm and <u>fore</u>knowledge

3 Remember that you can help yourself to learn several words for the effort of learning one if you make a habit of learning words in their noun – verb – adjective – adverb families, e.g. *memory, remember/memorise, (im)memorable, memorably.*

Write the following words in the IPA into appropriate places in the table (in normal script). Then complete the table. Remember that there may be more than one word in each box and in some boxes, it may not be possible to write anything at all.

'frendʃɪp 'frendli ə'prentɪsʃɪp fɔː'wɔːnɪŋ
prə'praɪətəʃɪp 'wɪtʃkrɑːft daɪəgrə'mætɪk
'dedli 'kɒstli

4 Choose six words that you would particularly like to learn from Exercises 2 and 3 and write sentences of your own using them in such a way that their meaning is illustrated.

Noun	Verb	Adjective	Adverb	

Speaking: Story-telling game

1 You are going to play a board game in groups of three to four people. Your teacher will give you a copy of the board you will use. The game also requires fifty-six cards or pieces of paper of about the same size as the squares on the game board.

You need:
– 4 cards with *Once upon a time* written on them.
– 4 cards with adjective + the word *ending* written on them, e.g. *happy ending.*
– 8 cards with a type of person written on them, e.g. *a ballet dancer* or *a robot.* These cards should have a little heart on them.
– 8 cards with objects written on them, e.g. *some jewels* or *a thunderstorm.* These cards should have a diamond on them.
– 8 cards with a general activity written on them, e.g. *arguing* or *chasing.* These cards should have a triangle on them.
– 8 cards with places written on them, e.g. *a forest* or *a ship.* These cards should have a circle on them.

Your teacher will give you some of these cards already prepared but some will still require you to write something on them.

Discuss with your group what to write on each card. Remember that what is written will provide the stimulus for stories and so it should give plenty of scope for the imagination.

When you have prepared your game, exchange your cards with those prepared by another group.

2 You are now going to play the game using the other group's cards. Your teacher will tell you the rules of the game.

3 When you have played the game once or twice, get into pairs with someone from the group who were playing with your group's cards. Tell each other the story or stories which your groups invented and discuss how successful the game was.

Speaking: A word game party

1 Work in groups of three or four. You are going to organise a word game party for the students in your own and another class of approximately the same level. Follow these instructions.

1 For this party you need about six word games. The games should all be ones which help students to practise their English in some way.

2 Choose the games you are going to play. You may choose any games that you wish from those you have worked on in this unit, but at least one game should be a different one suggested by someone from the group.

3 Plan the games thoroughly. For example, if you decide to play 'Just a Minute' or 'Twenty Questions', make a list of suitable subjects to be talked about or guessed.

4 Try out any games suggested by other students in the group and not already talked about in this unit.

5 Each person in the group should write out the rules of one or more of the games you chose. If you chose either 'Just a Minute' or the story-telling board game, don't write out the rules as they have already been presented fully in this unit.

6 When you have finished, compare your programme with those prepared by other students in the group.

7 Choose the most interesting 'new' game (the one which you feel provides the most useful practice for your English) from those suggested by the groups and try it out in class.

8 Invite another class to a word game party, using the games you have planned.

I spy with my little eye!

The main
aspects of
language
worked on in
this unit are:

- using computers for communicating
- writing – being brief and to the point
- present forms of the verb
- the language of e-mail
- universal vocabulary exercises

Warm-up: Communicating through computers

Discuss the questions below with two or three other students.

a What do you understand by the phrase 'the IT revolution'?

b List six different ways in which there has been a revolution in communications recently.

c How has this revolution affected you and your family or friends?

d Does the IT revolution bring both advantages and disadvantages? List what for you are the main advantages and disadvantages of the changes brought about by the IT revolution.

Reading: Computer information

1 The following text is about e-mail, an increasingly common way of communicating through computers. It is from the first pages of a computer manual.

What kind of points would you expect the first part of an e-mail manual for beginners to include?

Now read the first part of the text. To what extent was the content as you expected?

```
┌─────────────────────────┐
│   Romeo,,love           │
└─────────────────────────┘

      To:  Romeo
    From:  Juliet
 Subject:  love

Dear Romeo
Come to my balcony
tonight at ten
Juliet
```

The least you need to know

I have a friend who insists on telling me the 'good parts' of all the movies he sees, thus ruining these scenes for me when I get around to seeing the film. I've tried to stop him but you know how it is; some people are just plain incorrigible. If, like me, you prefer not to know the good bits beforehand, then you may want to skip this chapter.

On the other hand, if you're someone that likes nice, neat summaries that capture the gist of whatever topic you're dealing with, then, hey, have I got a chapter for you! What I'll be doing is running through a Top Ten list of questions that new e-mail users ask most. Each of these questions is answered in more detail in other parts of the book, but this chapter gives you some snappy answers to satisfy your curiosity.

What is electronic mail?

Electronic mail, or e-mail as it's normally shortened to, is just a message that is composed, sent and read electronically (hence the name). With regular mail, you write out your message (letter, postcard, whatever) and drop it off at the post office. The postal service then delivers the message and the recipient reads it. E-mail operates basically the same way except that everything happens electronically. You compose your message using e-mail software, send it over the lines that connect the Internet's networks and the recipient uses an e-mail program to read the message.

How does e-mail know how to get where it's going?

Everybody who's connected to the Internet is assigned a unique e-mail address. In a way, this address is a lot like the address of your house or apartment because it tells everyone else your exact location on the Net. So anyone who wants to send you an e-mail message just tells the e-mail program the appropriate address and runs the *Send* command. The Internet takes over from there and makes sure the missive arrives safely.

2 Now read the rest of the text. Answer these questions when you have finished reading.

a What do you think is the reason for the various bits of netiquette which are mentioned?
b What major problem is there with e-mail? Would this be a problem for you?
c At which points does the writer express an opinion rather than just giving straight facts?
d Why might some people disagree with his point about no 'powers-that-be'?
e Do you agree with him or not on this point?

What's this netiquette stuff I keep hearing about?

The Net is a huge, unwieldy mass with no 'powers-that-be' that can dictate content or standards. This is, for the most part, a good thing because it means there's no censorship and no one can wield authority arbitrarily. To prevent this organised chaos from descending into mere anarchy, however, a set of guidelines has been put together over the years. These guidelines are known collectively as netiquette (network etiquette) and they offer suggestions on the correct way to interact with the Internet's denizens. To give you a taste of netiquette, here are some highlights to consider.

➤ Keep your message brief and to the point and make sure you clear up any spelling slips or grammatical gaffes before shipping it out.
➤ Make sure the *Subject* lines of your message are detailed enough so they explain what your message is all about.
➤ Don't SHOUT by writing your missives entirely in upper-case letters.
➤ Don't bother other people by sending them test messages. If you must test a program, send a message to yourself.

⇒

What's a flame?

The vast majority of e-mail correspondence is civil and courteous, but with millions of participants all over the world, it's inevitable that some folks will rub each other the wrong way. When this happens, the combatants may exchange emotionally charged, caustic, often obscene messages called *flames*. When enough of these messages exchange hands, an out-and-out *flame war* develops. These usually burn themselves out after a while, and then the participants can get back to more interesting things.

Is e-mail secure?

In a word, no. The Net's open architecture allows programmers to write interesting and useful new Internet services, but it also allows unscrupulous snoops to lurk where they don't belong. In particular, the e-mail system has two problems: it's not that hard for someone else to read your e-mail, and it's fairly easy to forge an e-mail address. If security is a must for you, then you'll want to create an industrial strength password for your home directory, use encryption for your most sensitive messages, and use an anonymous remailer when you want to send something incognito.

3 Answer these questions about the content of the text.

a Imagine you are a complete newcomer to e-mail (so much the better if you really are). Is everything the writer says clearly understandable to you?
b What is the writer going to do in the rest of this chapter?
c At the beginning of the extract the writer mentions a Top Ten of questions. So far, the text has only dealt with five of these. What other questions about e-mail do you think you might want answered in this chapter if you were a complete newcomer to the subject?

4 Answer these questions about the style of the text.

a The writer uses a very colloquial and chatty style. Find at least five examples of this.
b Why does he use such a style?
c Is this the kind of style you expected, given the subject-matter?
d How do you feel about such a style?
e Write a summary of the information in the text. In other words, include only the information, ignoring any extra remarks. Write in a neutral rather than an informal style.

Grammar: Present forms of the verb

1 Look at the text about e-mail again and answer these questions.

a Which verb tense is used almost all the time in the text?
b Why is this the most frequent tense used?
c What other tenses are used in the text and why are they used?

2 This exercise checks your deeper understanding of the four present forms of the verb in English – the present simple, the present continuous (or progressive), the present perfect simple and the present perfect continuous.

Fill in the blanks in the sentences below. Discuss your answers in pairs. When you have agreed on your answers, see which pair got the highest number of correct answers.

a The .... form of the verb is used to describe something that is always true (e.g. a scientific law). For example, *Water .... if you .... it to 100ºC.*

b The .... form of the verb is used to describe something that is happening at this very moment. For example, *We .... an exercise on the use of the present tenses in English.*

c The .... form of the verb is used to talk about something that started in the past and is still true now. For example, *........................ President of the USA for .... years.*

d The .... form of the verb is used to emphasise the length of time that something has been going on – it started in the past and is still happening now. For example, *I .... English for .... years.*

e The .... form of the verb is used to describe the contents of a picture or photo. For example, *If you look closely at the picture, you can see that Jack .... Mary's hand.*

f The .... form of the verb is used to describe what happens in a book, play or film. For example, *At the end of the film, the hero and the heroine .... and they .... happily ever after.*

g The .... form of the verb is used to tell someone about the plans you have noted down in your diary for the next weeks or months. For example, *In July I .... a week at a conference in New York.*

h The .... form of the verb is used to give information about departure and arrival times of trains, buses, planes, etc. For example, *Flight NZ 145 .... in Heathrow at 10.50.*

i The .... form of the verb is used, with the adverb *always*, to comment on something which happens regularly but which irritates you. For example, *My car .... always .... down.*

j The .... form of the verb has a strong association with the words *since* and *for* + a time phrase. For example, *We .... each other since our schooldays.*

k The .... can be used to tell a joke or a story (the past simple is the most common form used in story-telling, of course). For example, *The waiter .... him a bowl of soup with a fly in it.*

l The basic sense verbs (*taste, smell, sound, feel, look*) are almost always used in the present .... form. For example, *Those flowers .... fantastic.*

m The verb *hear* is almost always used in the present .... form except in the following context: *The judge .... their case tomorrow.*

n The verb *see* is almost always used in the present .... form except in a context like the following: *I .... a sales rep tomorrow so I'll order some then.*

o The verb *think* is very rarely used in the present .... form except in the context of a guessing game. For example, *I .... of a word beginning with H.*

If you look closely …

At the end of the film …

Those flowers …

3 Follow these instructions.

1 Write three sentences describing this picture using the appropriate tense.
2 Write a couple of sentences describing the plot of a film you have recently seen on TV or at the cinema.
3 Write down two definite plans you have for the future, using the appropriate tense.
4 Write down exactly what you are doing at this moment.
5 Write down three true sentences about yourself using the present perfect tense (simple or continuous).

Listening: Surfing the net

1 You are going to listen to someone being interviewed about their experiences with the Internet. The person interviewed is asked the following questions. What do you think his answers might be? Discuss with a partner.

a When and how do you spend time on the Internet?
b What are some of the most interesting or curious places you have explored on the Internet?
c How do you feel when exploring the Internet?

2 📟 Listen to the recording once. Discuss the following questions with the same partner.

a Did you predict anything correctly?
b How did the person answer each of the questions? Note down all the points that you remember.

3 📟 Listen to the recording again. As you listen, add anything extra to the notes you made in the previous exercise.

Vocabulary: The language of e-mail

When sending e-mail it is considered important to be brief and to the point. Brevity can be partly helped by using abbreviations.

1 E-mailers also keep their messages brief by abbreviating frequently used phrases – through using just the initial letters of each word. Here are some commonly used abbreviations. They have been partially decoded for you.

Can you complete the 'translation'? They are all, of course, common phrases.

a AAMOF   as a m............... of f...............
b AFAIK   as f............... as I k...............
c FYI   for your i...............
d FYA   f............... y............... am...............
e IMO   in my o...............
f IOW   in o............... words
g NRN   not r............... necessary
h TTYL   talk to y............... l...............
i FAQ   f............... a............... question(s)
j BTW   by t............... w...............

2 A number of special computer words may be familiar to you from your general knowledge of English. However, these words have a different meaning in a special computer context.

Look at each of the words below and:

a explain what its meaning is in a special computer context.

b explain what its meaning is in a more general context.

c explain the connection between these two meanings.

Example: *flame*

a An abusive message to someone on the Internet.

b Something hot and burning in a fire.

c Both meanings of *flame* refer to something painful and destructive.

	computer meaning	general meaning	connection
mouse			
to surf			
the Net			
the Web			
drive (noun)			
a program			
hardware			
to load			
to paste			
a menu			
a virus			
a bug			
memory			

Writing: Being brief

1 Would you describe the text at the beginning of this unit as brief or not? Why/Why not?

2 In some types of writing, it is particularly important to be brief and to the point, whereas in others it is not especially important at all. Look at the list of types of writing. For which of these is it necessary to be brief?

instructions   faxes
love letters   adverts
news reports
insurance claims
short stories
scientific reports   e-mail
curricula vitae   poems
business proposals

3 Here are some more extracts from the *Complete Idiot's Guide to Internet E-Mail*, the source of the *Reading* text at the beginning of the unit. Write each one in a briefer fashion, cutting out everything that is not essential to the basic information being given.

a First off, let's get the boring definition of the Internet out of the way. The Internet is (yawn) an international collection of networks.

b As I mentioned before, busy e-mail readers often use the contents of the Subject line[1] to make a snap judgement about whether or not to bother reading a message. (This is especially true if the recipient doesn't know you from Adam.) The majority of mail users hate Subject lines that are either ridiculously vague (such as 'Info required' or 'Please help') or absurdly general (such as 'An e-mail message' or 'Mail') and they'll just press their mail software's 'delete button' without giving it a second thought.

R		Lisa green	4:46 pm	15/8/97	+	2	Meetings
		Katherine Miller	2:14 pm	16/8/97		4	New series
		James Hilton	2:53 pm	16/8/97	–	1	Payment
R		Carlos Dorado	11:12 am	17/8/97	+	11	Re: advances
•		Geraldine Stewart	12:09 pm	17/8/97		2	address
•		Peter Matthews	4:42 pm	17/8/97	+	2	trip

c Let's say you're schmoozing at some highfalutin' cocktail party and you meet someone who could send a lot of business your way. Dreams of new powerboats dance in your head as they say 'Here's my card. E-mail me and we'll do lunch.' You look at the card and – groan! – they have an MCI[2] mail address! Now what? Or suppose you're a CompuServe user and your best buddy has just gotten an Internet e-mail account. How on earth are the two of you supposed to make digital contact? These kinds of scenarios are increasingly common because, while there are tens of millions of people exchanging mail on the Net, there are tens of millions more who use other systems such as MCI Mail, CompuServe and America Online.

d Flame wars ignite for a variety of reasons: derogatory material, the skewering of one sacred cow or another, or just for the heck of it. One of the most common reasons is someone misinterpreting a wryly humorous, sarcastic or ironic remark as insulting or offensive. The problem is that the nuances and subtlety of wry humour and sarcasm are difficult to convey in print. You know your intent, but someone else may see things completely differently. To help prevent such misunderstandings, and to help grease the wheels of Net social interaction, cute little symbols called smileys (or more rarely emoticons) have been developed.

e Use passwords[3] that are at least eight characters long. Short passwords are susceptible to programs that just try every letter combination. You can combine the 26 letters of the alphabet into about twelve million different five-letter word combinations, which is no big deal for a fast program. If you bump things up to eight-letter passwords, however, the total number of combos rises to 200 billion, which would take even the fastest computer quite a while. If you use twelve-letter passwords, as many experts recommend, the number of combinations go beyond mind-boggling: 90 quadrillion or 90,000 trillion!

[1] a line at the top of an e-mail message used to indicate what the contents of the message are about.
[2] people get e-mail addresses either by using the Internet or by subscribing to different commercial servers like MCI, CompuServe and America Online.
[3] Sometimes it is only possible to read your e-mail by first typing a password.

4 E-mail messages usually have the following format:

To: (Name and e-mail address of recipient)
From: (Name and e-mail address of sender)
Subject: (Indication of main point of message)

Here is an example of an e-mail address:

smith@cup.ac.uk

Note that the symbol @ in an e-mail address is read as *at* and that the full stops are read as *dot*. Thus the example address would be read as *Smith at C-U-P dot A-C dot U-K.*

The ac.uk in the example address tells you that the address is based at a university in the United Kingdom.

Do you know anyone with an e-mail address? If so, dictate it to other students in the class. If not, then your teacher will give you some addresses for dictation.

5 E-mail messages must be brief in content.

They usually use a rather chatty, informal style, similar to that used by the writer of the text you have been studying in this unit.

They also sometimes make use of the symbols mentioned in extract d called 'smileys' which can be written using keys on the keyboard. They need to be read by tilting your head to the left.

Here are some examples.

:-)	Your basic smiley. This is used to mean *I'm happy.*
;-)	Winking smiley. *I'm flirting or being ironic.*
;-(	Frowning smiley. *I did not like something.*
:-I	*I am indifferent.*
8-)	*I wear glasses.*
:-{)	*I have a moustache.*
:-~)	*I have a cold.*

Here are some more smileys. Can you match them to their meanings listed below?

%-)   (-:   I-I   :-Q   :-@
:-D   <:-I   (:)   [:-)

a I am a dunce.
b I am an egghead.
c I am asleep.
d I am laughing.
e I am left-handed.
f I am screaming!
g I am wearing a Walkman.
h I'm sticking my tongue out at you.
i I've been staring at this screen for too long.

6 Write an e-mail message on paper to the student whose name the teacher gives you. Use an appropriate format and a chatty style. Try to use at least one smiley and some of the abbreviations studied earlier in the unit.

When you receive an e-mail message from someone write a response to it.

Continue writing messages until the teacher tells you to stop.

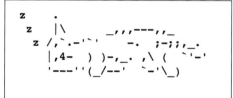

Let sleeping dogs lie …

C=:^)	head cook, chef-de-cuisine
Q:^)	soldier, man with beret, boy scout
*:O)	clown face; *I am feeling like a buffoon*
:^9	licking the lips; *very tasty or delicious*
/\/\/\/\O:>~	snake (or to rake someone over the coals)

Study skills: Universal vocabulary exercises

For most advanced students, one of the most important priorities in English study is to improve their vocabulary. You can do this in a passive way by simply reading English or listening to it for pleasure. However, it is a good idea to set yourself some vocabulary exercises on any text you find that is of particular personal or professional interest to you.

This is easy to do because there are a set of vocabulary exercises which you can use with almost any text that you wish to work on. It would not be a good idea to do all the exercises with any one text. Just choose two or three exercises which focus on the aspect(s) of vocabulary which you wish to work on.

Try some of these universal vocabulary exercises with vocabulary from the extracts of computer information or from the tapescript of the interview with the computer enthusiast.

1 Guessing from context

Underline three or more words which you do not know in the text. Try to work out their meaning, using their context and, perhaps, the structure of the word to help you. Check the meaning in a dictionary.

2 Grammar

a Choose three or more verbs in the text which you think might be useful to learn. Are they (a) regular or irregular, (b) transitive or intransitive (or both) and (c) what structures follow these verbs?
b Choose three or more nouns in the text which you think might be useful to learn. Are they countable, uncountable or both?
c Look at the prepositions in the text. Are these prepositions used because of their basic meaning or because they are in association with a particular word?

3 Collocations

a Find five adjectives and write down three nouns that collocate with each adjective.
b Find five transitive verbs and write down three objects that collocate with each verb.
c Find five nouns and write down three verbs that collocate with each noun either as the subject or the object.
d Are there any compound nouns or compound adjectives in the text? Write them down. Note down some other compound adjectives or nouns which share one part of the compounds found in the text, e.g. if you found *birthday card* and *big-eared* in the text, you could write down *credit card* (or *birthday cake* and *big-headed* (or *dog-eared*).

There are some more 'universal vocabulary exercises' in Unit 9.

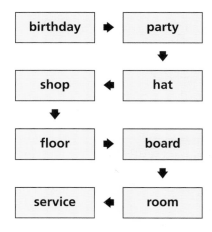

From another world
Travelogues

The main aspects of language worked on in this unit are:	• listening to travel accounts • affixes • speaking – making a presentation • noun phrases • speaking in public

Warm-up: Travel experiences

Work in pairs.

Take it in turns to talk for a minute about an important journey you have made – perhaps it was the first time you went abroad or perhaps it was a journey that was particularly difficult in some way. Do not interrupt your partner while he or she is speaking, just listen very carefully. After you have both spoken you may want to ask each other some questions about what you listened to.

Listening: My first time in Europe

1 ☞ Listen to the tape in which a speaker describes his first trip abroad. After listening, discuss the following questions with a partner.

a What do you learn about the speaker?
b What do you learn about his trip?
c The speaker mentions a number of things that struck him as being very different from home when he first arrived abroad. List all those that you can remember.

2 ☰ Listen to the tape again and notice how the speaker uses the adjectives below. Answer these questions.

a What is being described with each adjective?
b What point is the speaker making when he uses this adjective?

Example: *By using the word* skinny, *the speaker implies that he is no longer thin – middle age is usually accompanied by what is known as middle-aged spread and he suggests that this has happened to him. Skinny is also a negative word (in comparison with the more neutral word* thin *or the positive word* slim) *and so the speaker is generally presenting himself as a gawky, unattractive youth when he set out on this journey.*

skinny	grey	magical	steepled	undulating
endless	meandering	taut	ordered	fetching
smitten	unsliced	feathered		

3 Have you ever had the experience of being in a new place and noticing things in everyday life there that you had never seen before? If so, tell other students where you were and what you noticed there that surprised you.

Grammar: Noun phrases

A noun phrase is simply a collection of words focusing on a noun. It can be very short, as in *the countryside*; it can be slightly longer, as in *the unfamiliarly green countryside* or it can be considerably more complex, as in *that familiar countryside where I had grown up and which had moulded so much of my character*.

1 Underline all the noun phrases in the section which the teacher asks you to concentrate on in the article below.

Jumbo jet surgeon tells how he saved tourist at 35,000 ft

THE WOMAN whose life was saved in an emergency operation with a coat-hanger on board a jumbo jet flying at 35,000 ft left hospital yesterday after doctors said she was doing well.

Pauline Dixon, who collapsed with a punctured lung after being injured in a motor-cycle accident on her way to catch the flight from Hong Kong, was described yesterday by one of her saviours as 'an ideal patient'.

Mrs Dixon, 39, a mother of three from Aberdeen, would probably have died if she had caught the plane on which she was originally booked and the two doctors had not been aboard to help.

Brian Ellis, consultant surgeon at Ashford Hospital, west London, where Mrs Dixon was taken on arrival at Heathrow on Sunday, said, 'Without their action, they would have been taking a corpse off that plane.'

Professor Angus Wallace, an accident surgeon at Queen's Medical Centre, Nottingham, who answered an appeal for help on BA flight 052 with Dr Tom Wong, a junior doctor at Stracathro Hospital, Tayside, performed the improvised surgery using cognac, a coat-hanger, a roll of Sellotape and a bottle of mineral water.

Yesterday Professor Wallace described how he carried out the operation in row 53 of economy class. 'The woman was complaining of a painful arm. We made a makeshift splint and made her comfortable but after 20 minutes she said she had a severe pain in the left side of her chest.

'I examined her again and found she had between two and three fractured ribs. Her left lung had collapsed and was pressing onto the right one. I knew the situation could easily deteriorate. I realised we had to operate within five minutes.

'I told her I was terribly sorry but I was going to have to operate. She just smiled and said go ahead.

'The air crew were marvellous. Soon we had constructed a makeshift operating theatre around her seat, pinning up blue and red blankets for privacy. From the on-board emergency medical kit we got scalpel, scissors and a urinary catheter tube. We needed to make the tube rigid so a coat-hanger was pushed into it.

'We used brandy to sterilise the equipment. One of the stewards felt that if we were going to do it we should do it properly so a five-star Courvoisier was produced.

'I then made an incision and pushed the catheter into the chest wall. This was held in place with Sellotape and attached to a bottle of Evian mineral water to act as a chest drain.

'She was an ideal patient. She was apprehensive but she was quite ill, and often people who are quite ill accept what is being done to them. After the operation I must admit I had a rather large shot of brandy to calm my nerves. The patient gave me a kiss and a smile and said thank you.'

Dr Wong, back at Stracathro Hospital yesterday, declared he was 'delighted to help' but had played only a small part.

The professor's Nottingham colleagues were not surprised by his action. One woman doctor said yesterday, 'He is never a person to stand back if something needs to be done.'

2 **Comment on the noun phrases which you underlined. How long are they? How much extra information do they provide?**

Example: *The first noun phrase in the article (from the beginning of the text to 35,000 ft) takes up most of the first paragraph. It consists of a long relative clause summing up what happened and where it happened in the incident to be described in fuller detail later in the article.*

3 **Write down three adjectives which collocate with these adverbs. Use a dictionary to help you, if necessary.**

Example: seriously: *seriously ill, seriously injured, seriously rich*

a bitterly	**e** deeply	**i** utterly
b mildly	**f** pleasantly	**j** profoundly
c richly	**g** brightly	**k** desperately
d highly	**h** clearly	**l** incredibly

4 **Expand the underlined nouns in the exercise below in two ways. Firstly, add just an appropriate adjective or adverb + adjective. Then make the phrase slightly more complex by adding a phrase after the noun, and then make it considerably more complex by adding a clause.**

Example: We flew home on <u>a plane</u>.
We flew home on <u>a desperately crowded plane</u>.
We flew home on <u>a plane with only twelve seats</u>.
We flew home on <u>a plane of the same type as the one which crashed last week</u>.

a The <u>town</u> surprised me.
b We had a <u>time</u> there.
c My brother has just bought a <u>car</u>.
d We stayed in a <u>hotel</u>.
e I went to a <u>primary school</u>.
f I had a <u>friend</u>.
g My uncle worked for a <u>company</u>.
h A <u>family</u> moved into the house opposite ours.

Vocabulary: Affixes

1 In Unit 5 you did some work on affixes.

    a What is an affix?
    b From the text about the in-flight operation write down four words which contain affixes.
    c From the tapescript on page 169 find four more words using affixes.
    d What is the meaning of all the affixes which you have noted?

2 The affixes in the table below are all productive ones. In other words, they are often used today when new words are being coined. On the tape, for instance, you heard the speaker talking about *refuelling* the aircraft. You probably will not find *retranslate* or *re-elect* in your dictionary but if you saw them you would know immediately what they mean. If you want to invent a word meaning, say, mend for a second time, you would know that *re-mend* would be understood by your audience.

Complete the table by adding the meaning of the affix and think of two more examples of it in use. Although you may find some interesting examples of how these words are used in the dictionary, you may also be able to make up some examples of your own.

Affix	Meaning	Examples
arch-		arch-capitalist
bio-		biodegradable
co-		co-author
counter-		counter-offer
-ee		interviewee
-esque		Chaplinesque
ex-		ex-friend
-free		accident-free
half-		half-smiling
home-		home-distilled
hyper-		hyper-active
ill-		ill-chosen
inter-		international
intra-		intra-state
-ish		babyish
-ism		vegetarianism
-ite		Thatcherite
-less		characterless
mega-		megastar
mini-		mini-expedition
multi-		multi-talented
post-		post-election
pseudo-		pseudo-rustic
quasi-		quasi-autonomous
re-		refuelling
-rich		vitamin-rich
ultra-		ultra-capable

3 Which of the affixes in the table above could be combined with the following roots? Note that there may be several possibilities in each case and that you may be able to invent words which you will not find in any dictionary but which any native speaker of English would understand. How could the words you make be used?

    a Churchill   **d** intelligent   **g** project
    b college   **e** sugar   **h** affect(ed)
    c worker   **f** modern

Speaking: Making a presentation in public

1 Discuss the following with a partner.

a Have you ever had to speak in public? If so, when and why? How did you feel about it before your speech, while you were giving it and afterwards? What do you think you learnt that would help you to do better in future?

b What kinds of situations can you imagine where you might perhaps need to speak in public in the future (either in your own language or in English)?

2 Many people get worried when they have to speak in public. Discuss with a partner whether you think the following statements about speaking in public are true or false. Compare your ideas with those of other students.

a It is a good idea to write out your speech in advance and to read from a prepared script.

b Starting your speech with a joke will relax both you and your audience.

c You will feel more in control if you sit rather than stand while you are talking.

d You can improve your delivery by recording yourself as you practise your speech and then watching or listening to the recording critically.

e You will give a better speech if it is more spontaneous and less carefully planned in advance.

f You should make sure that you find out as much as you can about your audience in advance so that you can make your speech personally relevant to them.

g What you wear when speaking in public is very important.

h It can help to have a drink before you give your speech.

i It can help give you confidence if you imagine your audience are all chickens.

3 Here are some other pieces of advice but these have words missing. Fill in the missing words.

Making a speech in public can be a nerve-racking (1) .... but you will usually do it better if you are well (2) .... in advance. Think about (3) .... you want to say and about (4) .... you are going to say it. Plan your talk taking the interests and previous (5) .... of the members of your audience into (6) .... A talk on your experiences travelling in the USA is (7) .... to be rather different when given to an audience composed largely of North Americans (8) .... when given to a group of, say, schoolchildren from your own country.

When giving a speech, it is often (9) .... that speakers first outline (10) .... they are going to say, then say it in as much detail as is appropriate and finally (11) .... what they have said. You must address your audience clearly and without speaking too (12) .... or too (13) ....

It is often useful to have some kind of visual aid when giving your talk. You (14) .... like to prepare a handout or some OHTs ((15) .... projector transparencies).

4 📼 **Listen to two speakers. They are saying the same thing but one is much better at public speaking than the other. Which one is better and why?**

5 📼 **Follow these instructions to improve your pronunciation of English.**

1 Listen to the good speaker again and read the text (on page 169) aloud yourself at the same time as he is speaking.

2 Now read the text on your own, speaking as clearly as you can. Record your own voice if possible.

3 Then listen to yourself critically.

4 Improve your recording, if necessary.

6 **You are now going to practise giving a talk in your class. Follow these instructions.**

1 Choose one of the following topics for your talk:
   – an interesting place you have visited
   – something related to your own job or studies
   – an issue currently in the news

2 Prepare notes outlining your talk.

3 Prepare one, or possibly two, visual aids for your talk.

4 Give your talk to the class.

5 As you listen to each talk, note down two things that you liked about it and one thing that you felt could be improved.

Gather ye rosebuds
Poetry

The main aspects of language worked on in this unit are:
- enjoying poetry
- the grammar of poetry
- vocabulary for talking about poetry and the arts
- explaining opinions about works of art
- writing poems

Warm-up: Poetry

1 Discuss the questions below with a partner.

a What is a poem?

b What are appropriate subjects for poetry?

c Do you know any poems by heart (a) in your own language and (b) in English?

d What kind of poetry do you (a) like and (b) not like?

e Have you ever written any poetry? If so, what sort of poetry?

2 Here are some words which can be useful when talking about the techniques used by poets. Follow the instructions.

1 Check that you understand the meaning of each of these words. Use a dictionary, if necessary.

2 Invent an example for each.

rhyme
alliteration
simile
metaphor
repetition
onomatopoeia

Listening: Poetry

1 ☞ You are going to listen to a poem by Ogden Nash, a poet who lived from 1902 to 1971. The poem is on page 56. Some of the words are missing. Follow these instructions.

1 Discuss with a partner what you think the missing words might be. Note that lines 2 and 4 of each verse rhyme and so do lines 6 and 8. Use the rhyme to help you work out what the missing words might be.

2 Listen to the poem on the tape and check what the right words are.

Confession to be Traced on a Birthday Cake
by Ogden Nash

Lots of people are richer than me,
Yet pay a slenderer _____ (1);
Their annual levy seems to wane
While their income seems to wax.
Lots of people have stocks and bonds
To further their _____ (2);
I've cashed my ultimate Savings Stamp –
But nobody else has Frances.

Lots of people are stronger than me,
And greater athletic _____ (3);
They poise like gods on diving boards
And win their golfs and tennises.
Lots of people have lots more grace
And cut fine figures at _____ (4),
While I was born with galoshes on –
But nobody else has Frances.

Lots of people are wiser than me,
And carry within their cranium
The implications of Stein and Joyce
And the properties of _____ (5).
They know the mileage of every star
In the heavens wide _____ (6);
I'm inclined to believe that the world is flat –
But nobody else has Frances.

Speaking of wisdom and wealth and grace –
As recently I have _____ (7) –
There are lots of people compared to whom
I'd rather not be compared to.
There are people I ought to wish I was;
But under the _____ (8),
I prefer to continue my life as me –
For nobody else has Frances.

2 Summarise in one sentence what Ogden Nash is saying in his poem.

Is his message more effectively conveyed in verse than in your sentence? Why? Why not?

3 In the next poem which you are going to listen to, the lines have been mixed up. They are now in alphabetical order. Can you work out what the correct order should be? Use the rhymes as well as the meaning to help you.

Clues – It's in four verses of four lines each. The first line is f and the last is p. Also, lines 1 and 3 of each verse rhyme as do lines 2 and 4.

🔊 Listen to the tape. Did you work out the right order?

To the Virgin to Make Much of Time
by Robert Herrick (1591–1674)

a And nearer he's to setting.
b And this same flower that smiles today
c And while ye may, go marry:
d But being spent, the worse, and worst
e For having lost but once your prime,
f Gather ye rosebuds while ye may
g Old Time is still a–flying;
h That age is best which is the first,
i The glorious lamp of heaven, the sun,
j The higher he's a getting,
k The sooner will his race be run,
l Then be not coy, but use your time,
m Times still succeed the former.
n Tomorrow will be dying.
o When youth and blood are warmer;
p You may for ever tarry.

4 Summarise in one sentence what Robert Herrick is saying in his poem.

Is his message more effectively conveyed in verse than in your sentence? Why? Why not?

Vocabulary: The vocabulary of poetry

Poets are, by definition, particularly careful about their choice of words. We cannot, of course, be absolutely certain about what was going on in the poet's mind when he or she was composing. However, it can enhance our appreciation of their work to think about the effect which their selection of particular words has.

Consider the following questions on your own and then compare your answers with those of the rest of the class and the teacher. There are not necessarily any right answers to these questions.

1 Answer these questions about the Ogden Nash poem.

a What words does the poet use instead of these more common words:
  – brain   – lower   – shrink
  – grow   – rubber boots   – stand

b Why do you think Nash chose the words he did rather than the alternatives above?

c Ogden Nash in his poems often adds to the effect of his writing by using both common collocations (sometimes even clichés) and combinations of words which surprise because they are not normally used together. Which of the sets of words below frequently collocate and which do not?
  – income waxes
  – ultimate Savings Stamp
  – athletic menaces
  – cut fine figures
  – properties of uranium
  – wide expanses

2 Answer these questions about the Robert Herrick poem.

a Why do you think the poet chose the word 'rosebuds' rather than any other flower?
b Why 'smiles' rather than 'blooms'?
c Why 'glorious' rather than 'beautiful'?
d Why 'age' rather than 'time'?
e Why 'blood' rather than 'flesh'?
f Why 'still' rather than 'will'?
g Why 'lost' rather than 'passed'?

3 Find an example of each of the following in one or other of the poems above.

  – alliteration
  – simile
  – metaphor
  – repetition
  – onomatopoeia

Grammar: Grammar in poetry

In poetry you often come across grammatical forms and usage which you rarely meet in prose. This is sometimes because we still read poets from past generations when the grammar of English was not exactly the same as it is now. It can also, however, be because poets are able to take liberties with grammar. They can use what is known as 'poetic licence'.

1 Look back at the two poems at the beginning of the unit. Answer these questions.

a Does Ogden Nash do anything with grammar which strikes you as unusual? If so, what does he do and why do you think he does it?

b How does the grammar of the Robert Herrick poem differ from the standard grammar of twentieth-century prose?

2 📼 Here are some well-known verses. Listen to them read on the tape. Then, in each case, comment on the poet's use of grammar.

a What has he done that would be unusual in modern English prose?

b Does this affect the impression which the poet conveys in any way?

A

> Tell me not, sweet, I am unkind,
> That from the nunnery
> Of thy chaste[1] breast and quiet mind
> To war and arms I fly.
>
> (RICHARD LOVELACE, 1618–57)

[1] pure

B

> They name thee before me,
> A knell[2] to mine ear;
> A shudder comes o'er me –
> Why wert thou so dear?
> They know not I knew thee,
> Who knew thee too well; –
> Long, long, shall I rue[3] thee,
> Too deeply to tell.
>
> (Lord Byron, 1788–1824)

[2] bell rung to mark someone's death
[3] regret

C

> Only a man harrowing clods[4]
> In a slow silent walk
> With an old horse that stumbles and nods
> Half asleep as they stalk.
>
> Only thin smoke without flame
> From the heaps of couch-grass,[5]
> Yet this will go onwards the same
> Though Dynasties pass.
>
> Yonder a maid and her wight[6]
> Come whispering by:
> War's annals[7] will cloud into night
> Ere their story die.
>
> (Thomas Hardy 1840–1928)

[4] breaking up and turning over the earth
[5] type of wild grass
[6] young man (dialect word)
[7] recorded events

Speaking: Reciting poetry

1 Follow the instructions to help you read the poem of your choice effectively.

1 Which of the complete poems in this unit do you like best – the Ogden Nash or Robert Herrick poems from the beginning of the unit or the Thomas Hardy poem from the previous exercise?

2 Work with a partner who likes the same poem best and discuss what you particularly like about it.

3 Make sure that you fully understand the poem you have chosen. Use a dictionary or ask your teacher for help where necessary.

4 Read the poem aloud together with the speaker on the tape.

5 Practise reading the poem aloud in any way that you and your partner choose. You may, for example, wish to read the whole poem aloud in unison or you may prefer that one of the pair should read some sections and the other the rest. Decide what would be most effective. Ask the teacher to listen to you to help you perfect your reading.

6 When you feel happy with your performance make a recording of it or perform it in front of the rest of the class.

Vocabulary: Talking about poetry and the arts

1 Here are some adjectives which you might find useful when you want to talk about whether you like or dislike a particular work of art. Mark the words that express a positive emotion with a P and those that express a negative emotion with an N.

> appalling   appealing   astounding   banal   brilliant
> compelling   enchanting   engrossing   evocative
> intriguing   mediocre   moving   profound   repulsive
> ridiculous   spectacular   striking   stupendous
> superficial   thought-provoking   trivial

2 Complete the following sentences in any way you like. The first one has been done for you as an example.

a I usually find *Agatha Christie's detective stories* engrossing because *I am always anxious to discover who did it.*

b In my opinion, ... is a brilliant singer. I particularly like ....

c One of the most thought-provoking books I have ever read is .... because ....

d .... is a very evocative poem. It really captures ....

e To my mind, ... is a banal film whereas .... is much more profound.

f I find .... a very intriguing painting. I am fascinated by ....

g I thought .... was an appalling film because ....

h One of the most moving songs I've ever heard is .... It appeals to me because ....

3 Work with a partner and think of six other adjectives which could be used to describe your feelings about works of art. Try to think of both positive and negative words. Compare your lists with those of the rest of the class.

4 🔲 Songs are one of the most popular kinds of poetry. Listen to the song on the tape and follow these instructions.

1 Write down the words of the song.

2 Can you find any examples of rhyme, alliteration, simile, metaphor, repetition or onomatopoeia in the words of the song?

3 Which of the words you discussed in Exercises 1 and 3 might you use when talking about this song?

Writing: Poetry

Why not try your hand at writing a poem? It can be a very satisfying and enjoyable way of using language and some particularly original and effective pieces of work can be produced by people whose first language is not English.

The easiest way to start can be either to write something with a very clear structure or to base your writing on a picture or photograph. Try one or more of the following four exercises.

1 *Acrostics* are poems where the first letter of each line reading downwards forms the subject of the poem. Here is an example.

Leaping and flying
One made of two
Vowing and sighing
Ever to be true

Write an acrostic based on the name of someone you know – a friend, a teacher or a famous person.

2 A *haiku* is a form of poem originating in Japan. It consists of three lines, the first and third with five syllables and the second with seven. It can be a very effective form of poetry for capturing an image in a memorable way. For example:

Snowman in a field
listening to the raindrops
wishing him farewell.

Write a haiku about one of the following:

a a month of the year;
b something you experienced yesterday;
c a person you love.

3 A *limerick* is a humorous five-line poem with a characteristic rhythm and an 'a a b b a' rhyme scheme. It always opens 'There was a' followed by a reference to a person of or from a particular place. Read these limericks and answer the questions underneath.

There was a young lady of Ryde
Who ate some sour apples and died.
The apples fermented
Inside the lamented,
Made cider inside 'er inside.

There was a young man of Bengal
Who went to a fancy dress ball.
He went just for fun
Dressed up as a bun,
And a dog ate him up in the hall.

a How many syllables are there in each line of each of these limericks?
b How many stressed syllables are there in each line of each of these limericks?
c Calling the unstressed syllables short and the stressed syllables long, the first line of the first limerick could be described as 'short long short short long short short long'. How would the rest of the lines of both the limericks be described in this way?

Prepare for writing a limerick by thinking of as many words as you can which you could use for rhymes with the following place names.

> Rome   the States   Peru   Hong Kong   your home town
> any place of your choice

Now write a limerick about a person from one of these places using some of the rhyming words you have thought of. Remember to use the same rhyme scheme as in the examples of limericks and the same rhythm (i.e. pattern of stressed and unstressed syllables).

4 You can also often find inspiration for a poem from a picture or photograph. Look carefully at the picture and answer these questions.

a What can you see in the picture?
b What do you think the people in the picture are feeling? Why?
c How does the picture make you feel?

Write a poem based on the picture as a whole or on one aspect of the picture. Alternatively find a photograph of your own. Look at it and try to recapture how you were feeling when the photo was taken. Write a poem based on the photograph.

Speaking: Justifying your opinions about works of art

This exercise is an extended speaking activity called Arts Competition. Your teacher will give you instructions for it.

The main aspects of language worked on in this unit are:

- understanding a current affairs programme
- making a current affairs programme
- degrees of formality in spoken English
- collocations
- more universal vocabulary exercises

Warm-up: Current affairs programmes

1 A current affairs programme is a type of radio or TV programme which provides fuller information about one or more subjects of topical interest than is possible in an ordinary news programme. Answer these questions.

a Have you listened to or watched a programme of this kind recently (in any language)?
b If so, what topics were covered?
c If you had listened to a programme of this type this morning, what topics do you think might have been discussed?

2 The extract you are about to listen to is from part of a series devoted to National Energy Week.

Before listening, complete the chart below. Add one more source of energy and complete the other columns. Some boxes have already been filled in to help you.

Source of energy	Where it is obtained	How it is obtained	Advantages	Drawbacks
coal	coal mine	by mining		
oil				
nuclear power				potentially dangerous; expensive
solar power			cannot be used up; no pollution	
hydro-electric power				

3 The subject of the extract you are going to listen to is natural gas in Morecambe Bay in England. Before listening, look at the map to see where Morecambe Bay is and follow the instructions below.

1 Suggest three people who might possibly be interviewed in a broadcast on the subject of natural gas off the British coast.
2 Write down four questions which the interviewer might want to ask in relation to this topic.
3 Predict ten words or expressions which you think might come up in a current affairs item about natural gas in Morecambe Bay.

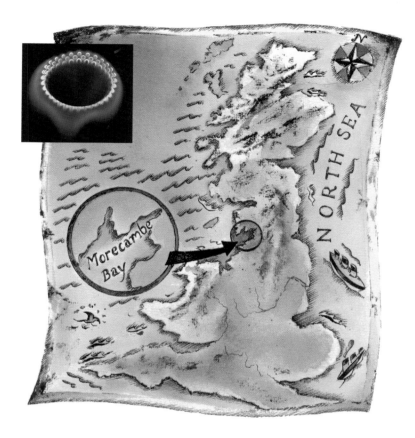

Listening: Current affairs

1 🔊 The extract comes from a current affairs programme called *Today*, broadcast every weekday morning on BBC Radio 4. Follow these instructions.

1 Listen to the first part of the programme and take notes on what you hear.
2 Compare your notes with those taken by another student. Do your notes contradict each other at all? Did you write things that your partner did not manage to catch and vice versa?
3 Listen again and correct or add to your notes if necessary.

2 🔊 Listen to the next part of the programme and take down what the speaker says as dictation. You have part of the script below to help you.

Oh, we have gas which I'm sure …
The history of exploration around the world …
I think we can look forward …
So we shall have to …

3 🔊 Now listen to the last part of the programme and take notes on what you hear.

4 How many of your predictions about the content and the vocabulary of the broadcast were accurate?

"Now we're going to talk about energy."

Grammar: Degrees of formality in spoken English

1 Answer these questions about the degree of formality of language used in the broadcast.

a How formally or informally did each of the speakers in the current affairs programme speak? Look at the tapescript on page 169 to help you decide.

b Why do you think they chose to speak in this way?

c Do speakers in your own language vary their use of formal/informal language in the same ways that English speakers do? In other words, are they formal or informal in similar situations and does the language change in similar ways?

2 Here are some examples of spoken English written down. As you read the extracts discuss these questions with a partner.

a How many people are talking in each case?

b Who are they talking to and what are they talking about?

c How formal or informal is the use of English?

d What aspects of the language helped you to decide on the degree of formality of the language used?

i)

'… you made a mistake ordering the tea if I may say so they just can't do it here I've been coming to this hotel for twenty years and I always bring my own tea bags of course it's changed a lot that new bit where you're staying used to be a field with a few goats and there was an old man selling sponges on the far side of the road his son now owns the taverna by the chemist's but you don't want to go there we got a terrible gippy tummy one year after eating the seafood salad no the best restaurant is a bit out of town it's a bit difficult to find actually I'll draw you a map if you like ooh you made a mistake buying those espadrilles in the hotel if you don't mind me saying so they saw you coming you should have waited until market day which is next Wednesday except you'll probably be gone on the Tuesday did I see you signing up for the all-day coach excursion? that isn't any good they say you're going to see the caves but you never get there you should go on the boat I know the captain he'll take you out to the island which has wonderful snorkelling and he cooks a meal on the boat of course he doesn't start doing it 'til next month because of the weather you've had bad luck with the sun haven't you? you always get the wind this month it's called the Maltropa oh no I wouldn't come here at this time of year …'

ii)

'Ladies and gentlemen, pray be upstanding to welcome our speaker for this evening, Lord Cherry of Fulbourn.

Lord Cherry is a graduate of this university who embarked on a distinguished career of service to the nation immediately after coming down with a double first forty years ago. Secretary of State for Education for two periods both marked by remarkable achievement, he has been described as the best prime minister we never had. Ladies and gentlemen, I give you Lord Cherry.'

iii)

'Please come and finish the game now.'

'You know that French student with the sort of nose rings, the one in Roland's class?'

'Roland's handed in his notice.'

'Please come now. You said you would.'

'You never. He's only just started!'

'Wonder if they'll replace him?'

'Stop pulling my clothes. I'm talking to Jill.'

3 The following features have been mentioned by grammarians as being particularly common in spoken rather than written English.

- continuous or progressive forms of the verb
- long, wandering and loosely connected sentences, sometimes unfinished
- long noun phrases introducing the subject of a sentence
- use of hesitation devices (*sort of, I mean*, etc.)

To what extent can you find these characteristics in each of the examples of text in Exercise 2? Look at the tapescript on page 169 and at the three reading texts.

Can you suggest why these features are or are not found in these texts? Do you think that similar features would be found in the spoken version of your own language? Why/Why not?

4 Extract i) in Exercise 2 was from a series called *Great Bores of Today* published in the satirical magazine *Private Eye*.

This series of articles is usually written almost without any punctuation, as in 2 i). Why do you think they are written in this way?

Mark where the speaker would pause for breath – or where there would be a full stop or a comma if the extract were punctuated in the normal way.

Imagine you are acting the part of the speaker in text i). Read out the words in the way which you feel is most appropriate for the part.

5 The series *Great Bores of Today* always presents monologues on subjects that are likely to irritate the listener. They are often topical in some way – something recently in the news, a current TV programme, the weather at the time of year.

▣ Listen to some people talking in the style of this series, *Great Bores of Today*. Can you identify what topics they are each talking about?

Can you imagine any other topics that might have provided a theme for an article in this series?

6 With a partner write a monologue for inclusion in the *Great Bores of Today* series. It should be on some aspect of one of the following topics:

- energy sources
- the current government (of your own or any other country) or some figure in it
- one of the ideas suggested by the class in Exercise 5.

Follow these instructions.

1 Imagine who is speaking and in what kind of situation. The situation could be, for example, at a party, in school, at the family dinner table, whatever you wish.

2 Try to use each of the features of spoken grammar mentioned in the introduction to Exercise 3.

3 Take it in turns to read your monologue to the rest of the class. The other students should guess what the subject of the monologue is, what kind of person is speaking and in what situation.

Vocabulary: Collocations

1 Below are some collocations from the various texts you have been working on in this unit. Write some other collocations for all the underlined words in the examples. The first one has been done for you as an example.

a <u>staggering</u> development
staggering news; a staggering blow; a staggering improvement
b <u>nuclear</u> power
c a <u>straightforward</u> operation
d a <u>distinguished</u> career
e <u>tea</u> bags
f <u>all-day</u> coach excursion
g to <u>misinterpret</u> data
h to <u>hand in</u> one's notice
i the demand <u>increases</u>
j a final <u>question</u>
k tea <u>bags</u>
l a distinguished <u>career</u>
m market <u>day</u>
n nuclear <u>power</u>
o to misinterpret <u>data</u>

2 Look at any other items of vocabulary which you have written down while working on this unit. Add some collocations to any of these where appropriate. For example, if you have written down *current affairs*, you might add:

current issue of a magazine; of current interest; current opinion; international affairs; family affairs; business affairs.

Speaking: Current affairs

You are going to make an item for a current affairs programme. Work in groups of four to six students and follow these instructions.

1 Decide what subject your item is going to focus on. Here are some suggestions:
  – a social issue that is of current concern to the students in your class
  – a new (imaginary) invention
  – a famous person or event
  – a special place in the town where you are studying
2 Plan your programme. Make sure you include:
  – some introductory remarks
  – at least two interviews with some interesting questions
  – some concluding remarks
3 Decide who is going to take responsibility for each bit of the item. Then work individually or in pairs on your bit of the item, doing any research or other work that is necessary before you are ready to make the programme.
4 Practise what you are going to do.
5 When you are happy with your proposal, record your item or write it out on paper.
6 If you recorded your programme, play it to the rest of the class. If you wrote it out, act it out to the other students.

Study skills: Universal vocabulary exercises

Here are some more universal vocabulary exercises of the type you looked at in Unit 6, i.e. exercises which can be used with vocabulary from any text. Try these exercises with vocabulary that you would particularly like to focus on from this unit.

1 Word formation. Find five words from the unit that you would particularly like to learn. Write them in the appropriate box in the table below (one word on each line). Now complete the table with other parts of speech from the same root. Remember that it may be possible to have more than one word in each box – an abstract noun and a person noun, for example, or an adjective with an opposite formed with a prefix. It may, however, be impossible to complete some of the boxes.

Noun	Verb	Adjective	Adverb

2 Grouping words. Follow these instructions.

1 Choose 10 words from the unit that you would particularly like to learn. Arrange them in two or three groups in any way that you like.

2 The main topic of this unit is current affairs. Find five examples in the unit of words relating to that topic. Then think of five other words to add to a collection on that topic.

3 Register. Follow these instructions.

1 Choose one text from the unit – a listening or a reading text. What register is it in – formal, informal, neutral? Is there any kind of specialised register in the text e.g. medical or technical?

2 Find three words or expressions in the text that reflect its register.

The main aspects of language worked on in this unit are:

- reading short stories
- writing a narrative
- tenses in narrative
- clichés

Warm-up: Ideal partners

1 What do you think a story called *The Perfect Pair* might be about?

Read the first part of the story. Were you right in your interpretation of the title?

The Perfect Pair

A True Story

Nobody was at all surprised when Katie Mulholland and Alex Mustoe announced their engagement. They had been inseparable for more than four years, clearly loved each other, and were of the perfect age to get married, Katie being twenty-six and Alex four years older. Each time they went away on holiday together – to Sardinia, Tobago, or skiing in Zermatt – their friends predicted, 'Katie and Alex will come back engaged this time'. And eventually they did, which gave everyone the double satisfaction of being proved right, as well as boundless and genuine delight for the couple.

2 Before reading any more of the story, discuss the questions below with one or two other students.

a What do you think makes a married couple or a boyfriend/girlfriend partnership deserve to be called a perfect pair?
b Who do you know who best fits the description a perfect pair? Why do they fit the description?

3 Most of the story is about Katie and Alex's wedding day. What do you already know about English wedding customs?

Reading: The Perfect Pair

1 Read the next section of the story and then draw a quick sketch of Alex and Katie.

Katie and Alexander were in every respect a perfect pair. Both were blond, amiable and pleasant-looking. Alexander had a wide face, tightly curled hair and an engaging grin. Although he never said anything remotely memorable, or expressed an opinion that differed from those of his friends, he was charming, good-humoured and relaxed. During the day he worked as a financial analyst for a firm of City stock-brokers, but he seldom mentioned it. His real pleasures in life, one felt, came from his holidays, his friends and from Katie.

Katie Mulholland was, beyond a doubt, an ideal match for Alexander Mustoe. She was that rare thing, a genuine English rose, small and slender and sweet-natured with perfect fair skin, blue eyes and a pointed little nose like a miniature dog. Her blonde hair, which she sometimes tied back with a black velvet bow, was thick and straight. Like Alexander, there was nothing introspective about her. She had learnt to regild picture frames and had set up a little business in a workshop in Pimlico, which she shared with two other girls and a busy telephone. Unless they were hectic, she rang Alex every afternoon, to make plans for the evening. 'Katie's what I call a really nice girl,' her friends' mothers would say. 'One day, she's going to make a wonderful bride.'

2 Read the next part of the story and follow the instructions below.

Alex Mustoe had a flat in a mews in South Kensington opposite Christie's in the Brompton Road and it was here that he and Katie did most of their entertaining. Katie's flat in Dawes Road, which she shared with her sister, was rather small, so she prepared the food for their dinner parties in her little kitchen and drove it over to Alex's. They were disciplined hosts and invited people for dinner once a fortnight. When they were invited anywhere, they always paid back. Katie cooked the first course and the main course, and Alex always made one of his specialities: bread and butter pudding or Greek yoghurt with a spoonful of cherry jam. Once a year, in June, Alexander gave a drinks party to which he invited the same people. The list hardly varied from one year to the next. It didn't bother him: these were his friends.

Hanging in the bathroom of Alex's flat were two enormous framed collages that Katie had made from old holiday photographs. The faces of their numerous friends smiled out at them. John and Mark and Alice and Tiggy in Ischia; Philip water-skiing in Corfu; Annie painting her toenails on the caique; Vicky off-piste. Katie and Alex liked to go on holiday in a group of friends, especially if Willie Buchanan was in charge. Willie was Alex's oldest friend and a great team leader, so they were always pleased when he rang to say he'd booked a chalet for a week in Courchevel or taken a villa sleeping ten with a tennis court in Portugal. His handsome dark face was all over the collage. When Katie and Alex got engaged it was obvious that Willie would be the best man.

1 Summarise with a partner what you have learnt so far about the lives and characters of Alex and his fiancée.
2 Choose two or three words or expressions from this section of the story which you would particularly like to learn.

3 ☐ **Listen to the next part of the story on the tape.**

What do you learn in this part of the story about what kind of wedding it is going to be?

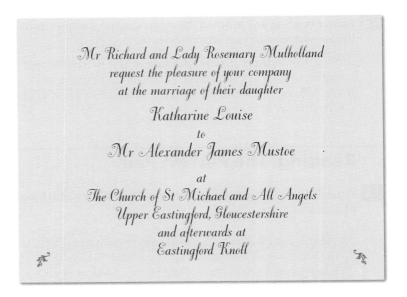

*Mr Richard and Lady Rosemary Mulholland
request the pleasure of your company
at the marriage of their daughter*

Katharine Louise

to

Mr Alexander James Mustoe

at

*The Church of St Michael and All Angels
Upper Eastingford, Gloucestershire
and afterwards at
Eastingford Knoll*

4 Now read the next part of the story. Match the wedding photos below to the section of the text which they relate to.

Now the bridesmaids were lining up in the porch: four little girls in white dresses with yellow sashes and ballet shoes. Each was clutching a posy of buttercups and daisies which matched the yellow and white theme of the flowers in the church, and around their necks were the little sand pearl necklaces that Alexander had given them yesterday at the rehearsal, as bridesmaids' presents. 'What sweet bridesmaids,' every single person said as they went into the church. 'How lovely it is to be at a proper country wedding.'

Inside the church, the village organist doodled inconsequentially with his stops in, while a phalanx of tall athletic ushers squeezed more and more guests into the pews, like guards on the Tokyo underground.

At two minutes past three, there was a flurry of activity at the back of the church, and the dazzle of flashbulbs that announced the arrival of the bride. And then the organist struck up with 'Praise my soul, the King of Heaven' and Katie began her solemn procession down the aisle – small, slender, sweet-natured Katie, who had never looked quite so lovely as she did at that moment, with just that hint of smugness in her face that brides have, as she held on to her father's arm and her four pretty bridesmaids scuttled along in her wake, holding onto her train. The congregation sang lustily, slow to chide and quick to praise, and whispered to each other how beautiful Katie looked.

And so the wedding proceeded: Katie making her vows in a surprisingly strong voice for such a slight girl, which made her older relations swell with pride. Willie Buchanan – taller and sleeker than ever – produced the wedding ring on cue, which was duly blessed and Alexander James and Katharine Louise were pronounced man and wife. The vicar of St Michael's, who had known Katie since she was ten or eleven and had prepared her for confirmation, gave a short, old-fashioned address, in which he mysteriously likened Alexander to the captain of a village cricket team and Katie to the opening batsman and wicket keeper combined. Psalms were sung, then 'Love divine, all love excelling', the wedding party disappeared into the vestry to sign the register, and finally Alexander and Katie reappeared to the strains of 'Jerusalem' and processed back down the aisle, smiling and waving at John and Mark and Alice and Tiggy as they swept by.

At Eastingford Knoll nothing that is conventional at a traditional wedding reception had been neglected.

Guests arrived at the front door of the house, were directed through the Mulhollands' drawing room and out through french windows into a pink and white striped marquee on the lawn. The grass had been covered by yards of coconut matting, and ranged along the billowing walls of the tent were round tables decorated with baskets of pink and white roses. A score of ladies from the village handed round glasses of champagne, triangles of bread with smoked salmon, asparagus rolled in brown bread, and rather delicious sausages on sticks with Dijon mustard. The pretty little bridesmaids soon kicked off their shoes and ran around the tent playing tag and shrieking. Elderly stubble-cheeked men in tailcoats swayed up to Katie saying, 'You don't know me, but I'm an old, old cousin of your husband's. Alexander's certainly a lucky chap, and I wonder whether I might take the liberty of kissing the bride?'

At the end of the tent was a small raised dais – a couple of feet high – on top of which was a three-tiered wedding cake, thick with royal icing and garlanded with orange blossom, and white freesias. Here stood Alex and Katie – Katie radiant as she stood beside her still-nervous husband – to cut the cake with Richard Mulholland's Brigade of Guards sword. And here too they were joined by Katie's favourite godfather and sleek Willie Buchanan, to make their speeches on behalf of the bride and groom.

5 🖭 **What sorts of things do you think the bride's godfather usually says in his wedding speech? Listen to Katie's godfather making his speech and answer the questions below.**

a What sorts of things did Katie's godfather say in his speech?
b How do you think Katie's mother will be feeling at this moment? She planned the wedding: is everything going as she would have wished?

6 It is now the groom's turn to speak. Read the next part of the story and answer these questions.

    a This section marks the beginning of a change in the story. In what way?

    b Has Alex said anything that would surprise the wedding guests?

And only now as he stepped towards the microphone, did the grey and strained look of the bridegroom begin to register with the crowd. I had vaguely noted his tension during Gerry McNeill's speech – indeed throughout the day – but such were the high spirits of the bride, and the widespread feeling of goodwill, that it had been easy to overlook it.

But one could not now ignore his gaunt expression; there was a tautness about Alexander's mouth and an emptiness about his eyes that was chilling. And though he mustered a smile as he took his place at the microphone, there was no joy in it.

'Er, ladies and gentlemen, I'd like first of all to propose a toast to our bridesmaids,' said Alexander dryly, looking down at the four pretty little girls in yellow sashes, clustered around the cake. 'If I wasn't already married to the most wonderful girl in the world, I'm sure I'd like to be married to one of our gorgeous bridesmaids today – Davina, Janie, Lucy and Jemima. Ladies and gentlemen – the bridesmaids.'

'The bridesmaids,' responded the crowd, and took another deep sip of champagne.

'So many people,' went on Alexander, 'have taken such trouble to make today a success that I hardly know where to begin. The vicar, of course, the Reverend Philip Goode, and Mrs Phipps and Mrs McGuire who arranged the stunning flowers in the church, and Mrs, er' – he momentarily consulted the piece of card in his hand – 'Mrs Spence, who produced the delicious food here at the reception. Thank you all very much indeed for all of this. And more than anyone, of course, I want to thank Katie's mother, Rosemary, who has been the brilliant general behind the scenes and really has organised everything so meticulously today. If Lady Rosemary was at the helm, England really would have nothing to fear!' At which joke the crowd laughed jovially, and a little cheer went up for Rosemary Mulholland and her sterling powers of organisation.

Now that he was underway, Alexander spoke more confidently, and it was only the deathly-white pallor of his skin, and a certain deadness about his eyes that gave one the slightest cause for concern.

'And next, of course,' he went on, 'I want to thank my best man, Willie Buchanan.' He turned toward Willie, who was standing, feet apart, a glass of champagne in his hand, a yard or two to Alexander's right. Knowing that the eyes of the crowd were all on him, Willie smiled modestly and ran his hand through his thick brown hair.

7 ▭ Now listen to the end of the story and follow these instructions.

1 Summarise what happened in this last part of the story.
2 When Alexander's ushers spoke to him, what other options were open to him?
3 Why do you think he chose to behave in the way he did?
4 Does the writer finish the story at a good point or should he have told us what happened next?
5 What do you think might have happened next?

Grammar: Tenses in narrative

1 Which tense is the main tense used in this story?

Comment on the tense used in the following extracts from the story. Why is this tense used here?

a 'Katie's what I call a really nice girl,' her friends' mothers would say.
b 'One day she's going to make a wonderful bride.'
c On the grass verge outside the church, and all along the village street, cars were parking and doors slamming. Girls were adjusting their hats and men who had driven down from London were pulling on their tailcoats. It was ten minutes to three and the bells of St Michael's Church were pealing loudly.
d John and Mark and Alice and Tiggy had been lunching at the Red Lion on the village green and now hurried towards the church to bag a decent pew.
e When Katie and Alexander had come to draw up their lists for wedding invitations, they realised to their dismay that they'd need to ask about three hundred people; they had so many friends and their parents had insisted on so many relations and friends of their own.
f They would be hard pressed to fit everyone in the church.
g 'Willie has been my best friend for twenty-two years since we both arrived at preparatory school in the same term.'
h 'I do want to say that over the years, we've had some great times together.'
i 'I realised if my new girlfriend couldn't get along with my best friend, then the relationship was going to be doomed from the word go.'
j 'Fortunately, Katie did approve of Willie.'
k 'These are two return tickets for the Maldives where Katie and I were going to spend our honeymoon.'
l 'Under the circumstances, Willie, I think it would be more appropriate if you had them.'

2 Think about what you were doing at midday yesterday. Then write a paragraph about that time using as many different verb tenses as you can.

Example: *At midday yesterday I was sitting in the dentist's chair. I had been sitting in the waiting room for over half an hour and had been getting more and more nervous. So I was quite relieved when I was called into the surgery. I was only going to have a check-up and so there was no real reason to feel nervous. But I've always hated going to the dentist and, even though there's no need to be afraid these days, I still am …*

Vocabulary: Clichés

1 Discuss the following with other students in the class.

a Can you define what a cliché is?
b Can you give any examples of clichés?

2 Do you need to a) know and b) use clichés? Why/Why not?

Read the text before answering this question.

If we wish to avoid saying anything precise, then clichés are what we need. Such wishes are commonplace. It is not possible to be fresh and imaginative all the time. Life is full of occasions when a serious conversation is simply too difficult, or too energetic, and we gratefully fall back on clichés. They can fill an awkward gap in a conversation; and there is no denying that there are some conversations that we would rather not have. In such circumstances, clichés are an admirable lexical life-jacket. The passing remarks as people recognise each other in the street but with no time to stop, the self-conscious politeness of strangers on a train, the forced interactions at cocktail parties, or the desperate platitudes which follow a funeral: these are the kinds of occasions which give clichés their right to be.

No one would be satisfied with clichés when we expect something better from a speaker or writer. A politician who answers a direct question with clichés can expect to be attacked or satirised. A student who answers a teacher's question with a cliché is, we hope, not going to get away with it. Likewise, we complain if we encounter poems, essays or radio talks filled with clichés. But a blanket condemnation of all clichés is as futile as unthinking acceptance.

3 Here are some of the clichés from Alex's speech used in a different context. In each case a word is missing. Fill in the missing word and, where appropriate, identify the situation from which the cliché was originally drawn.

a Mrs Thatcher was at the .... in British politics for thirteen years.
b They never liked each other from the word ....
c We don't see so much of each other now that she's gone up in the ....
d The success of the village concert is thanks to those who put in so much work behind the ....
e Everyone wished the bride and groom the very best for their .... lives together.

4 ▭ You are going to listen to a collection of clichés gathered together in one text for humorous effect. You have the text below but with one word missing in each of the clichés used. In each case you are offered three alternatives. Follow these instructions.

1 Read through the text quickly. Choose which word you think is needed to complete each of the clichés before listening to the text.
2 Listen to the text and check your answers.

If I may venture an (1) opinion/idea/interest ...., when all is said and (2) made/done/gone ...., it would (3) badly/ill/poorly .... become me to suggest that I should come down like a (4) load/barrow/ton .... of bricks, as large as life and (5) twice/half/big .... as natural, and make a (6) hill/mountain/storm .... out of a molehill on this issue. From (7) years/time/ages .... immemorial, the object of the (8) game/play/exercise ...., as sure as (9) bacon/eggs/chickens .... is eggs, has been first and (10) foremost/last/best ...., to take the bull by the (11) tail/ears/horns ...., and spell (12) that/everything/it .... out, loud and (13) strong/high/clear .... That's it. Take it or (14) find/lose/leave .... it. On your own (15) back/hands/head ...., be it. All (16) nice/good/bad .... things must come to an end. I must (17) love/miss/kiss

.... you and leave you. I (18) tease/kid/trick
.... you not. Don't (19) ring/call/phone
.... us, we'll call you. And I don't (20) say/think/
mean .... maybe.
    Am I (21) wrong/left/right .... or am I right?

5 Choose eight of the clichés from the text above that you would
like to learn and write them down in a context which illustrates
their meaning more clearly – each one could either be in a
sentence or in a dialogue.

Writing: A narrative

1 Discuss the questions which the teacher gives
you with a partner.

2 Work in pairs and follow these instructions.

  1 Choose one of the real or imaginary
situations you have been discussing and think
some more about how you could develop it
into a full length story. You can move as far
away from the incident you discussed as you
wish.

  2 Jot down some ideas about the story.
    – Who are the main characters going to be?
What do they look like?
    – How is the story going to be told? In the first
person by a minor participant? Through the
eyes of one of the major characters? By an
unnamed observer from above?
    – What are going to be the major events of the
story?
    – At what point in the narrative should the
story begin? And when should it end?
    – Where is the story going to be set? What
details about the setting need to be given?
    – How are the feelings of the participants
going to be revealed? Through their words?
Through their behaviour? Through a
straight description of how they felt?

  3 When you have each got some notes on paper,
talk through your ideas with your partner. Ask
each other about points that you may not be
sure about and possibly modify your plans in
the light of your discussions.

4 Write your story. Try to use the following
aspects of language which have been referred
to in this unit:
  – variety of tenses e.g. past continuous to set
the scene and past perfect to describe
something that had previously happened
  – direct speech
  – interesting adjectives
  – language which appeals to other senses
than the visual e.g. sounds and smells.

5 Exchange stories with your partner. Comment
on the content and accuracy of each other's
work. Make any appropriate changes.

6 Read stories written by other students in the
class.

7 Decide which of the stories you read are based
on a real incident and which on an imaginary
one. Check whether you were right or not
with the original author.

The main aspects of language worked on in this unit are:	• understanding public speeches • speaking – rhetorical devices • the unreal past • idioms and their origins • speaking with a tape

Warm-up: Public speeches

1 🔊 Listen to six short extracts from speeches on the tape. For each speaker decide:

a on what occasion the speaker is speaking;
b what characteristic elements of the speech helped you identify the occasion in each case;
c what special technique(s) he or she is using.

2 Can you think of any other situations when public speeches may be made? Share ideas as a class.

3 Discuss the following questions with two or three other students in the class.

a What professions frequently involve making public speeches?
b What kinds of purpose can public speeches have?
c Have you ever heard anyone (in any language) making a particularly effective public speech?
d What did they do or say that made their speech particularly impressive?
e Can you think of any other things a speaker can do to make his or her speech memorable for the audience?

Compare your group's answers to these questions with those given by other students in the class. List all the techniques you can think of on the board. Note that such techniques can be referred to as rhetorical devices.

4 These phrases are typically used in speeches. Identify when they might be used.

a Ladies and Gentlemen
b Unaccustomed as I am to public speaking
c Please raise your glasses
d I ask you to join me now in toasting
e Three cheers for
f I leave you with the thought
g Shakespeare put it well
h It is my great pleasure to address you here today on the occasion

Listening: A political speech

1 ▭ Every year all the major British political parties hold a conference where party members get together and discuss areas of interest. You are going to listen to a speech by the leader of a political party, Jo Grimond. Listen to the introduction to the speech and answer these questions.

a Which party was Jo Grimond leader of?
b What else are you told about Jo Grimond?
c How long after the Second World War was this speech made?

2 ▭ Listen to the speech. What is the main point that he is making?

3 ▭ Here is the first part of the speech with some words missing. Listen again and fill in the blanks.

War, (1) ...., war has always been a
(2) .... affair and in (3) .... days,
commanders were taught that, when in (4) ...., when
in (5) ...., they should (6) .... their
troops towards the sound of (7) .... I intend to
(8) .... my troops towards the sound of
(9) ....
    Politics are (10) .... And the fog of political
(11) .... can obscure many (12) ...., but
we will march always towards the sound of the guns. Our
(13) .... for too long has (14) .... not to
see what it does not like. It has put its telescope to the
(15) .... eye in a very un-Nelsonian
(16) .... It puts its telescope to the
(17) .... eye so that it can say that there is no
(18) .... in sight.

4 ▭ Now listen to the last part of the speech. Take down what you hear as dictation.

5 ▭ Listen to the speech again as you read the text on page 171. Then go back and correct any mistakes in your dictation. If you are not sure of the meaning of anything in the speech, then ask a partner if he or she can explain what you do not understand. If your partner is also not sure, then use a dictionary.

6 Discuss the following questions as a class.

a How effectively do you think the speaker makes his points?
b Did he make use of any of the rhetorical devices which you discussed in Warm-up Exercise 3?
c In Warm-up Exercise 3 you probably listed rhetorical devices which the speaker did not make use of. Would he have been able to use these devices in this speech, do you think? If so, how?

Grammar: Unreal past

The unreal past is a term used in grammar books to refer to a form which looks like a simple past tense but which is used to refer to either present or future time. Some people feel it is more accurate to call it a hypothetical present form. Whatever you like to call it, this form is often found in political and other public speeches aimed at putting across a strong opinion.

1 Look at the verbs in italics in these sentences taken from political speeches.

<u>It is high time</u> we *took* stock of the situation and *made* a determined effort to halt the damage before it goes any further.

<u>If</u> people *did not fear* the prospect of unemployment as much as they do, the trade union movement would be stronger.

<u>Supposing</u> you *were appointed* Prime Minister tomorrow, what would your first act be?

Everyone <u>wishes</u> they *had* more time to help.

<u>If only</u> time *didn't fly* past so quickly!

We <u>would rather</u> the government *spent* more on the underprivileged members of society than that the rich *were protected* from paying higher taxes.

I <u>had sooner</u> we all *had* to work that little bit harder than that the country *went* to the dogs.

Answer these questions.

a What tense are all the verbs in italics?
b What time are they referring to – past, present or future?
c Why do you think there is this mismatch between form and time reference?
d What tense would be used in these constructions if the time being referred to really was the past?

2 Write sentences beginning with the following phrases, but write about something that is referring to the past.

I wish I
If only the government
Supposing the Queen

3 When are each of the phrases underlined in Exercise 1 mainly used? Put each of them in one or more of the following categories:

– frequently used in everyday chat between friends;
– characteristic of formal speeches;
– used in informal writing (e.g. personal letters or popular journalism);
– used in formal pieces of writing (e.g. business reports or academic texts).

4 Work with two or three other students and follow these instructions.

1 Think of two or three social, economic or political issues which are controversial in your country at the moment.
2 Discuss what you think the government should do to try to deal with these issues.
3 Write sentences giving your opinions about the issues you chose. Your sentences should begin:
It's high time
If
Supposing
We wish
If only
We would rather
We had sooner
4 Compare your ideas with those produced by other groups of students.

5 Think of how the following sentences could be completed.

a It's time the monarch
b I wish the government
c If only people
d Supposing the Prime Minister
e It is time that students
f I had sooner a few people
g We would rather the country
h It is high time the opposition

What different possibilities did other students in the class come up with for each of these sentences? In each case, write down the suggestion which you like best.

Vocabulary: Idioms and their origins

The idioms of a language can tell us a lot about the history and culture of the people who speak that language. As an island people, the English have a lot of idioms which have original associations with the sea and sailing. As both agriculture and warfare were major aspects of English people's lives in the past, so there are many idioms associated with these fields of activity. Similarly, all popular English sports have sparked off a number of idioms.

1 In his speech, Jo Grimond uses a number of metaphors and idioms. Match the idioms to the field of activity they originate from.

    a It puts its telescope to the blind eye …
    b It is against this enemy that we march.
    c … without passing through the furnace of defeat

> the army
> heavy industry
> sea-faring

2 Find the idioms in each of these sentences. Say what the idiom means in plain English and then explain how the idiom may have originated. The first one has been done for you as an example.

  a As soon as she mentioned his son, she realised that she had found the chink in his armour.
    the chink in his armour = his weak spot (*chink = hole*, i.e. the point at which he could easily be attacked, an image from fighting in the days when soldiers wore armour)

  b He was refused the promotion he was hoping for but at least they sugared the pill by offering him a better office. (Clue: children and medicine)

  c Bob looks tired. He must have spent the night on the tiles. (Clue: cats)

  d The day we met for the first time was a real red-letter day for me. (Clue: calendars)

  e It's time the government put some of its older ministers out to grass. (Clue: horses)

  f Jane is sailing rather close to the wind in criticising her boss so publicly. (Clue: yachting)

  g My father's not sorry to have retired from the cut and thrust of big business. (Clue: fighting)

  h When the chips are down, you discover who your true friends really are. (Clue: gambling)

  i Amanda often doesn't get home until the small hours. (Clue: numbers)

  j His uncle's getting a bit long in the tooth to go on adventure holidays, isn't he? (Clue: horses)

  k The baby cries. I get hardly any sleep and then get cross easily next day. The baby senses I'm upset and cries still more. It's a vicious circle. (Clue: logic)

  l If this experiment doesn't work, we'll have to go back to square one. (Clue: board games)

  m An election some time during the next three months is certainly on the cards. (Clue: fortune-telling)

a night on the tiles

out to grass

cut and thrust

3 Horoscopes in English popular magazines or newspapers are often rich in idioms. Underline all the idioms in your own section of the horoscope below. Again try to explain both the meaning and the origin of all the underlined idioms.

HOROSCOPE for the next 12 months!

Aquarius
(Jan 20 – Feb 18)

Your personal life is in for a bit of spicing up this year. Good times won't just be handed to you on a plate, though – you'll have to work hard for them. You will have to keep your nose to the grindstone because money seems to burn a hole in your pocket this year.

Pisces
(Feb 19 – Mar 20)

This year you are set to get more in tune with yourself and your own needs. You will move from being an underdog to becoming a prime mover in any project that you become involved in. Don't let it go to your head, however; a skeleton in your family's cupboard may emerge later in the year.

Aries
(Mar 21 – Apr 20)

Your usual Arian desire to take total control of everything will take a back seat this year while you settle for making just one section of your life run as smoothly as possible. Your financial fortunes are likely to fluctuate but you will manage to keep your head above water.

Taurus
(Apr 21 – May 20)

You like to take refuge from the hustle-bustle of the world in your own home but this year is the time to take the bull by the horns and to move on to fresh pastures. Spread your wings and you will never look back.

Gemini
(May 21 – June 20)

You will need to rely on your family to warn you when you are about to go off the rails this year. Listen to what they say or you could walk into the classic Gemini trap of setting yourself a target that is impossible to attain.

Cancer
(June 21 – July 22)

Take every opportunity to branch out in the first part of the year because, come the autumn, you will be having to play second fiddle to someone who has not yet entered your life.

Leo
(July 23 – Aug 22)

You will feel particularly resentful of commitments which eat away at your energy. Don't let days drift by when you could be packing them full of new opportunities.

Virgo
(Aug 23 – Sep 22)

Mid-October will bring an ongoing saga to a dramatic head. You may feel as if a victory which was within your reach has been cruelly snatched away. But you will soon become very much aware of the truth of the saying that every cloud has a silver lining.

Libra
(Sep 23 – Oct 22)

While some dreams produce psychological carrots which keep us doing donkey work long enough to get good results, others simply aren't worth losing sleep over. You will learn to tell the two apart this year.

Scorpio
(Oct 23 – Nov 21)

By the end of the year you'll be thanking your lucky stars for some of the best times you have ever experienced. A relationship may go through a rather rocky patch in May but otherwise every area of your life will receive an enormous boost.

Sagittarius
(Nov 22 – Dec 21)

This year you will start to point your life in a more fruitful direction. You will take big steps to improve your situation both at work and at home but do not run away with the idea that the entire year will be a time of intense inner drama. That is not the case.

Capricorn
(Dec 22 – Jan 19)

You will end the year with a clean sheet. So you should spend the months ahead preparing to tie up loose ends and to draw a clear line between your past and your future.

Study skills: Speaking with a tape

It can be a very good exercise in pronunciation to speak at the same time as a native speaker on a tape. You can only do this successfully if you do not overstress weak syllables and if you make your voice go up and down in the same way as the original speaker. Follow these instructions.

1 Read the tapescript and listen to the recording of Jo Grimond's speech again. Mark all the places where he pauses for breath.
2 Mark all the vowels which are pronounced with the unstressed /ə/ sound.
3 Practise reading Jo Grimond's speech with him!

Speaking: Making a speech and rhetorical devices

Follow these instructions and practise making a speech.

1 Individually prepare a slip of paper like this:
WHEN:
WHO:
WHAT:
2 Beside WHEN, note down one of the speech-making situations you discussed at the beginning of the unit. Beside WHO, note down who is speaking (e.g. the father of the bride, a head teacher). Beside WHAT, indicate what the speech should be about (e.g. best wishes for the newly-weds, some moral guidance for school-leavers). When you are ready, fold your slip of paper in half.
3 Shuffle the slips of paper and take one each. In groups of three or four students, compare your slips of paper. Discuss how you would approach each of the speeches. Think about the audience of the speech and its purpose and consider what it would be appropriate to say in the given situations.
4 Choose one of the speeches to work on in detail.
5 Write out the speech in full, remembering the audience and the purpose of writing as you prepare the speech. Try to include as many as possible of the rhetorical devices mentioned in the unit. Bear in mind also the points discussed on page 53 relating to making a public presentation.
6 Make notes summarising the key points from the speech.
7 Choose one person to give the speech. This person should give the speech using the notes rather than the words in full.
8 Give the speech to the rest of the class. The audience should:
   a say what they thought the WHEN, WHO and WHAT on the original paper were.
   b in the groups in which you prepared the speech, give each of the other speeches a mark out of five for
      – clarity
      – interest
      – achievement of purpose
      – use of rhetorical devices.
   This should lead to a possible total mark of 20.
9 Total the marks for each speech to see which group gets the Public Speaking Award for the class.

The main
aspects of
language
worked on in
this unit are:

- reading business reports
- writing – reports
- conjunctions and other linking words
- building business vocabulary
- revising your work

Warm-up: What are company reports?

1 With a partner discuss the
following questions.

a Why do companies
produce yearly and half-
yearly reports?
b What sort of impression
would these reports be
aiming to create?
c Would the reports always
tell the truth, the whole
truth and nothing but the
truth?

2 Imagine you are writing a
half-yearly report for the
past six months on behalf of
either the company you
work for or the school where
you are studying; note down
the main points you would
cover in your report.

Reading: Business reports

1 Here are some words which have been taken from the first part
of a company's half-yearly report to shareholders.

> although   however   particularly   increasingly   therefore
> where   who

Read the Chairman's statement from the beginning of the
report and insert the words in the correct places.

CHAIRMAN'S STATEMENT

The Group had an excellent first half with sales and profits considerably ahead of last year. Our performance was particularly strong when viewed over two years, with increases in sales and profits of 15.7% and 38.8% respectively.

The trading climate remains very competitive and consumers in all countries where we trade are cautious and value-conscious. (1) ...., we enjoy a close relationship with our suppliers (2) .... benefit from large volumes of production and

(3) .... they and we are well placed to contain higher raw material costs in our prices.

We continue to build on our traditional strengths of quality and value, using design and technological innovation to create (4) .... desirable ranges of clothing, home furnishings and food. The UK Outstanding Value Campaign remains effective and we extended this policy to Continental Europe (5) .... it had an immediate impact on the autumn sales performance.

We will continue to grow the business at home and overseas and are accelerating footage developments, (6) .... in the UK and Continental Europe. Group capital expenditure of over £400m will be at a record level this year.

The Group is in a strong position. (7) .... the second half of this year will not have the benefit of a 53rd week, I am confident that the year as a whole will show continued good progress.

---

2 Read the rest of the report and answer these questions.

a What non-financial information about the company is given?
b Does it sound like a good company to have shares in?

Half-year review

Group sales increased by 6.9% to £3.1bn and profit before tax increased by 15.1% to £354m.

An interim dividend of 2.8p per share (2.5p last year) will be paid in January.

United Kingdom

Sales increased by 6.3% to £2.5bn; operating profits increased by 15.7% to £343m.

Clothing sales increased by 8.9% to £1.3bn and continued to gain market share. The Company won the Classic Fashion category in the recent British Fashion Awards. This coincided with strong progress in sales of more fashionable merchandise. Sales of home furnishings decreased by 0.8% in a difficult market.

Food sales increased by 3.9% to £1.1bn in the face of fierce competition and without the benefit of an Easter trading week this year. Growth came from continuing product innovation, building on the Company's established reputation for quality, freshness and convenience.

Staff productivity improved and cost increases were well contained. UK profitability for the period increased to 13.6% from 12.5% last year.

A new edge-of-town store opened near Warrington, with 87,000 feet of selling space including a customer restaurant. In the year as a whole nearly 500,000 square feet will be added, of which two thirds will be in town and city centres, bringing the total UK footage to 11.1m square feet. The store chain continues to be modernised providing improved customer care supported by a number of service initiatives.

Now that Sunday trading is legal in England and Wales as well as in Scotland the majority of stores will open on Sundays in December this year. Approximately 30 stores are currently trading successfully on Sundays but it is too early to evaluate the impact of seven-day trading on sales and profits.

Growth in profits from financial activities came from Financial Services through an increase in personal lending and further improvements in the bad debt record.

Overseas

Despite the continuing recession in Continental Europe, sales in European stores (which now include the Republic of Ireland) increased by 13.2%. Operating profits were below last year largely due to higher pre-opening costs from the accelerated store expansion programme. A new store opened in Paris on Rue de Rivoli, and further stores open at La Defense in Paris, Valencia and Madrid during the second half of the year. The Outstanding Value Campaign is now established throughout Europe and significantly lower prices came into effect from the beginning of September. Sales since then have been well above last year's levels.

The stores in Hong Kong continue to achieve substantial increases indicating considerable potential for growth in the Far East.

Export sales to the Group's franchise operations around the world increased by 19.0%.

A UK Christmas trading statement will be issued in January.

3 Prepare some comprehension questions about the text.

1 With a partner, write six questions on the text to ask another pair of students. They may be questions that ask for explanations of things that you do not yourselves understand fully or they may be questions which you feel will test the other students' understanding of the text. You and your partner should both keep a copy of your questions.

2 Work with a different partner and ask each other your questions.

Vocabulary: Building business vocabulary

1 Information in company reports is often presented graphically, e.g. through a graph, a pie chart, a bar chart, an organigram or a table. What kind of graphical presentation is each of the following?

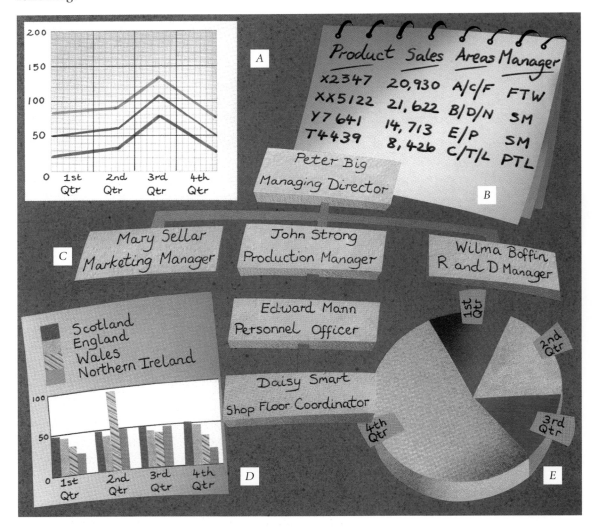

Give an example of how each of these might be used by a company or organisation you are familiar with.

Can you think of any ways in which some of the information in the report could have been effectively presented graphically?

2 Make a rough sketch of at least three of the following. Then compare your drawings with those of a partner. Ask questions of each other and comment on each other's drawings.

a A pie chart illustrating how you spend your leisure time.
b A bar chart showing how your use of your leisure time has changed over three distinct periods of your life.
c A table illustrating any numerical information you like about the members of your family (for example, their ages, their heights, the number of hours per week they spend at work/on housework, the amount of money per year they spend on clothes, etc.)
d An organigram for either your workplace or your school or college.
e A graph showing fluctuations in some aspect of your work or social life over the past twelve months.

3 Work with a partner on the business vocabulary in the text.

Go through both parts of the report underlining any other words or expressions which are of particular use in a business context. Check that you understand all the words and phrases you have underlined.

4 Complete the following business vocabulary word forks in any appropriate way. Some words are suggested in the box below but you will need to find some more of your own. Use a dictionary to help you, if necessary.

annual care deal
encourage figures
international launch
losses organise outlet
overall plan
production satisfaction
targets

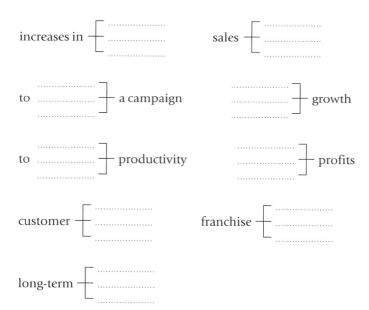

increases in

sales

to .... a campaign

.... growth

to .... productivity

.... profits

customer

franchise

long-term

5 ▭ Listen to the business news report on the tape and follow these instructions.

1 Note down any key items of business vocabulary which you hear.
2 Recount the business news you listened to. Try to use all the words you noted down.

6 Work with a partner and follow these instructions.

1 Choose three or four of the items of business vocabulary you noted down in Exercise 5 which you particularly want to be able to use.
2 Do a word fork for each of these items.
3 Compare your word forks with those prepared by other students. Make a note of any collocations which you feel are particularly useful.

Grammar: Conjunctions and other linking words

Cohesion is the linguistic term used to refer to the features of a text which show how words, phrases and sentences are linked to each other. The words which you put back into the first part of the business report in Reading Exercise 1 (*although, however*, etc.) are all examples of words used to produce cohesion in a text.

There are many ways in which cohesion is achieved in a text but two of the main grammatical ways are through the use of conjunctions like *although* or *because* and through the use of linking adverbial words or phrases like *moreover* or *in spite of this*. Words and phrases like these have been compared to signposts on a road or grid references on a map; they help the reader understand where he or she has come from or where he or she is going to.

1 *Although* is a conjunction; it joins two or more clauses to make a compound sentence.

1 As a class, brainstorm all the conjunctions you can think of.
2 In pairs, divide all the conjunctions your class thought of into groups. You may divide them into categories in any way that you like but, to help you, here are two group headings which you may find useful – *Time* and *Condition*.

2 *Moreover* is an adverb. It is used to make connections between sentences (or paragraphs) rather than clauses.

In pairs, think of two more adverbs or adverbial expressions which can be used to make the following connections between sentences or paragraphs:

a Time connections, e.g. *afterwards*
b Contrast connections, e.g. *on the other hand*
c Cause and result connections, e.g. *therefore*
d Sequencing connections, e.g. *firstly*
e Adding connections, e.g. *moreover*
f Drawing conclusion connections, e.g. *in conclusion*
g Giving example connections, e.g. *for example*

Compare the adverbs and adverbial expressions you thought of with those written by other students. Add any extra words or expressions to your own lists.

3 ▭ Listen to the tape. You are going to hear some incomplete sentences. Follow these instructions.

1 Write down what the speakers say.
2 Then complete their sentences in any appropriate way.
3 Compare your answers with those produced by other students.

4 Choose two or three of the cohesive words or phrases which your teacher suggests to you. These may be either conjunctions or adverbs. Follow these instructions.

1 Write sentences to illustrate each of the cohesive devices you chose.
2 Read your sentences clearly to other students in the class. Do not read the cohesive device out, however. Say *toot* instead.

3 The other students must guess what *toot* was replacing. Note that sometimes they may choose a word or phrase that would fit correctly and logically into your sentences even though it is not what you were thinking of. If they do this, they get two points but they must go on guessing until they guess what you had in mind (the first person to guess this gets five points). An incorrect or illogical suggestion gives the sentence reader an extra mark.

5 Here is an article from *The Financial Times*. A number of cohesive words or expressions have been removed from it and are in the box above the text. Read the text and fit the words back into it. One of the words or expressions listed is used twice.

largely   such as
however   also   in short
accordingly
on the other hand

AIR TRAVEL has always been regarded as a barometer of overall economic activity. .... (1), one has only to visit any airport in Europe or to study the statistics to be convinced that the recession of recent years is on the wane.

Not only are European airports becoming busier, but most of them are .... (2) undergoing modernisation and expansion. It has been estimated that the cost of worldwide aviation infrastructure modernisation could run as high as $350bn from 1991 to 2010 with airport development alone accounting for $250m of that, the rest being .... (3) for air traffic control facilities.

The figure, ... (4), covers basic development costs .... (5) terminals, runways, aprons and the necessary equipment for operations. It does not, ... (6), cover the cost of associated infrastructure developments .... (7) external road and rail links and other facilities which are often separately funded developments. .... (8), if these outlays are included, the overall cost of world airport development could be much higher, perhaps about $400bn.

6 Find a suitable newspaper or magazine article of your own and write out some sentences or paragraphs from it without the cohesive devices, as in Exercise 5. Make sure you write enough of the text down to make it clear which cohesive device fits logically. You will almost certainly need to look in a quality newspaper or a fairly serious magazine rather than in a tabloid newspaper or light magazine.

Write down the words and expressions you remove (in a different order) above the text. Keep a note of what the text originally looked like. Give your sentences or paragraphs to another student to see if he or she can work out where the words and expressions originally went.

Study skills: Revising your work

In Units 6 and 9 you looked at some universal vocabulary exercises, i.e. exercises to help you learn vocabulary which you could use with any texts you are working on. Those exercises were concerned primarily with understanding the meaning of new words and expressions and with learning how to use them and how to commit them to memory in the most effective way.

Psychologists say that we learn things properly only if we revise what we have learnt. The exercises here will help you to revise any vocabulary you have been learning.

The following exercises should be done at different times after working on the words and expressions – 10 minutes later, the following evening, 24 hours later, a week later or a month later, for example.

1 **For practice now try each exercise with some different vocabulary items from any of the first twelve units of this book. Later, use any of the exercises that you find particularly useful again with other words that you wish to revise.**

1 Choose ten words that you would particularly like to learn and write sentences using each of them in such a way that their meaning is illustrated.
2 Write a paragraph on a completely different subject in which you use as many as possible of the new words and expressions learnt.
3 Have a conversation with a friend in which you try to see how many of the words and expressions studied you can each use.
4 Close the book. Which of the new words and expressions learnt can you remember? What do they mean?
5 Re-tell one of the reading or listening texts – either orally or in writing – without referring back to it. Then read or listen to the text again.
6 Look back at any notes about vocabulary which you made during your studies. Read through them again. Then see how much you can remember of your notes, without looking at them. Read them through again and underline or highlight anything that you did not recall.
7 Write a paragraph for a learning diary in which you mention some of the most important words and expressions which you have learnt and explain why you feel those words and expressions are important for you.
8 Write the words or expressions on cards with their translation or other notes about them on the back. Test yourself by looking at the front of the card and trying to recall what is on the back.
9 Write sentences using each of the words and expressions which you want to learn in a different context from the one provided in the original text.

2 **You are now just over halfway through this book. Look back at what you have learnt so far. Write your teacher a letter saying what you have liked most about the course and about any particular problems you are having. If you have any suggestions about how you would like the second part of the course to go, now is a good time to make them.**

On the brain
Lectures

13

The main aspects of language worked on in this unit are:
- listening to lectures
- writing and speaking – expanding notes
- *-ing* form of the verb
- vocabulary of lectures
- taking notes

Warm-up: The brain

What do you know about the brain? Brainstorm with the rest of the class to see how much information you have between you.

Listening: Neuronal connections in the brain

1 🔲 Look at the illustrations and listen to a short extract from a lecture on the workings of the brain. Make notes as you listen.

2 Follow the instructions below.

1 Looking at your notes, write a short paragraph summarising the content of the part of the lecture you listened to.
2 Compare your paragraphs with those written by other students. What differences – if any – do you notice in terms of the content of what you wrote?
3 Listen again and amend your paragraph if necessary.

3 Here are some things which people giving effective lectures often do.

use visuals   give examples   draw analogies   make jokes
pose questions – then answer them
connect theory with practical illustrations
state what the lecture is going to be about at the beginning
summarise the main points of the lecture at the end
use connectors, e.g. *firstly*, *secondly*, *as a result*, etc.
rephrase an important point to make sure it is clear
quote authorities in the field

Look at the list of lecture techniques and answer the questions.

a Which of these is exemplified in the lecture you have just listened to?
b Can you think of any other effective lecturing techniques to add to the list?

Vocabulary: The vocabulary of lectures

1 Lecturers use terminology appropriate to their theme. Think about the lecture you have just heard and follow these instructions.

1 Write down as many such theme-related words and expressions as you can remember from the lecture.
2 Look at the tapescript on page 171. Can you add any words to your list?
3 Can you think of any other words which could usefully be added to such a list even if they were not used in this lecture extract?

2 Often words may be used in a range of contexts but they acquire a more specialised meaning when collocated in a particular way or when used in a particular context.

What words or expressions from the lecture you heard are needed to complete the gaps in the sentences below?

a The little boy didn't have any brain ....
b The little boy's eye was bandaged just at the .... time when the nerves were ....
c The normal eye made .... with its appropriate
....
d Nature .... a vacuum.
e You won't find any .... territory.
f Another factor in establishing neuronal .... is that neurones like to work.

3 In what ways could the words you used to fill the gaps in Exercise 2 be used in other more general contexts?

4 Here are some sentences from lectures on other disciplines. What discipline – e.g. astronomy, geography, sociology – does each sentence relate to? Underline the words and expressions which helped you to identify the discipline.

a I would like to begin by drawing your attention to the key factors which would eventually lead to the revolution. Firstly, there was considerable discontent with the reigning monarch who ruled as an autocrat but had lost the respect of many of his subjects …
b Could I now turn your attention to the key features of the glaciated landscape. This is characterised by, for example, rounded mountain tops, U-shaped valleys, corries, hanging valleys, moraine … Let us consider each of those in turn.

c … was also remarkable as a poet as well as a dramatist. He may be most famous for his thirty-seven comedies, tragedies and histories but he also wrote a large number of sonnets, not to mention several other longer poems.

d The possibilities of cyberspace are beginning to be more and more fully exploited. Gophers allow anyone with access to the web to retrieve information from all over the world. E-mail permits instant communication between people from opposite ends of the world, people who would never otherwise have met. Virtual reality is becoming part of everyday reality for more and more people.

e Very occasionally complications may develop as a result of an attack of measles. The physician needs to be aware of the fact that otitis media, pneumonia or, in a very few instances, encephalitis may occur with measles. The normal course of action is to prescribe antibiotics if any such complications are suspected.

f Computer corpora have greatly aided the work of lexicographers and have also made it easier to analyse how people actually do use language. In a number of cases this has enabled us to see that tenses are in practice used in rather different ways from those traditionally described by grammarians.

g Chelonia is an order of reptiles – 244 species in all. They are characterised by a body which is encased in a domed shell of bones covered by large horny scales.

h Torts are always dealt with in the civil courts. Individual torts include negligence, trespass and nuisance and the usual remedies are damages and/or an injunction.

5 What discipline have you attended most lectures on in English or your own language – or are you most likely to attend lectures on? Follow these instructions.

1 Write down ten nouns, five verbs and five adjectives associated with that discipline. Use a dictionary, if necessary.

2 Write down at least one appropriate collocation for each of the words you have written. For your nouns you might write a collocating adjective or verb; for your verbs you might write down either a subject or an object noun or perhaps an adverb; for your adjectives write down a suitable noun.

6 Other elements of the vocabulary of lectures are common to lectures whatever the discipline. For example, the word *factor* is often used in lectures on a range of topics. Make a collection of these. Follow these nstructions.

1 Look at the tapescript for the lecture extract which you listened to at the beginning of this unit on page 171 and make a list of any words or expressions which you feel may be commonly used by lecturers regardless of their discipline.

2 Look again at the extracts in Exercise 4 and add to your list any other general words and expressions useful for lecturers.

7 Here are some nouns frequently used by lecturers in any subject area. Divide the words into groups in any way that seems logical.

conclusion consequence diagram effect graph
hypothesis impetus influence issue objective OHT
outcome point principle rationale reason
significance slide system theory

8 Choose one of the words from the box in the previous exercise to fill each of the blanks in the paragraph on the right. Notice that one of the words is used in two blanks.

There are a number of (1) .... which you must bear in mind when considering the development of education throughout the Soviet period. Firstly, the writings of Marx were a significant (2) .... on those in charge of the new Soviet Ministries of Education. One of the basic (3) .... of Marxism was a faith in the (4) .... of a child's environment as opposed to his or her genetic make-up as far as educational achievement was concerned. Therefore, a main (5) .... of the new Soviet (6) .... of education was to provide every child with the best possible educational environment. Secondly, the need to transform the country into a major economic power also had a profound (7) .... on the development of Soviet education, providing the (8) .... for considerable financial investment in schools and other educational establishments. This investment may be the major (9) .... why Soviet education proved so successful in training world-class scientists. However, other scholars have put forward the (10) .... that the moral education programme was of great (11) .... here. Before considering the whole (12) .... of moral education in the USSR, I should like you to look at the first (13) .... On it you have a (14) .... – I hope you can see it at the back – showing the structure of the Soviet education system as it had developed by the early 1930s.

9 Write a paragraph of your own relating to any discipline that you are familiar with, using the seven remaining nouns from Exercise 7.

Read your paragraph to other students in the class. Can they guess what discipline you had in mind?

Grammar: *-ing* form of the verb

1 Look at these examples from the lecture of how the *-ing* form of the verb can be used and answer the questions below.

Let's have a look at him here having his eyes tested.
Here he is with a doctor doing extensive examinations on his eyes.
… the reason was – it was finally discovered on questioning the mother – that …

a In the first example who does *having* refer to?
b In the second example who does *doing* refer to?
c In the third example who does *questioning* refer to?

2 Join the sentences in each pair using an *-ing* form of one of the verbs.

Think about the meaning of what you are writing. Sometimes it will be necessary to use *being* or *having* + the past participle.

Example: Look at the boy. A doctor is examining him.
Look at the boy being examined by a doctor.

a In Cambridge there are many people. They work in the computer industry.
b The cherry trees are very beautiful. They flower in the spring at the same time as the daffodils underneath them burst into bloom.
c Every morning there are hundreds of cars with only one person in each of them. They block the roads and create terrible traffic jams.
d A new cinema is under construction on one side of Oxford Square. It will open next January.
e Ms Cox has written a number of sociology textbooks. She is well known in university social science departments.
f I have read *War and Peace* several times. I, therefore, feel I know quite a lot about life in Russia at the beginning of the nineteenth century.
g Teenagers today live at a time of great uncertainty. They are more likely to complain of finding life stressful than did young people of previous generations.
h Modern business people frequently have to travel for work purposes. They need to get from A to B at the greatest possible speed and with the least possible disruption.
i In this lecture I have considered a range of factors which have contributed to increasing crime in this country. I believe that the most significant of these is mass unemployment.
j It is now time to draw this lecture to a conclusion. I would like to reiterate that many of 'Shakespeare's plays' may indeed not have been written by Shakespeare himself.

The cherry trees are very beautiful

Terrible traffic jams

3 In the second example in Exercise 1 the *-ing* form was preceded by a noun to indicate who the action of the verb referred to. Express the sentences below in a more literary way – through the use of the words in brackets and the *-ing* form. In each case the *-ing* form will be preceded by a noun.

Example: I don't like it when people smoke in restaurants. (object)
I object to people smoking in restaurants.

Before doing this exercise you may find it useful to check that you remember how each of the words in brackets is used, e.g. *to object to doing.*

a The teacher always says that students must arrive in class on time. (insist)
b I am so sorry that my little boy is being so noisy. (apologise)
c Richard said how well behaved our children were. (compliment)
d It's your job to see that the rabbits get fed. (responsible)
e It's silly for Jack to spend so much time practising the guitar. (no point)
f It would be a good idea for Sandra to get an Apex ticket if she's got to go to Edinburgh next month. (worth)
g In my dream last night John was being chased by a wolf dressed up as a sheep. (dream *verb*)
h They didn't think it was amusing when Stella jumped on the table and started to dance on the tablecloth. (appreciate)
i More and more school-leavers do not manage to find jobs. (an increase)
j He will probably get the job if the manager is in a good mood at his interview tomorrow. (depend)

4 Take it in turns to ask a partner these questions. Answer in any way you like – as long as you use an *-ing* form of a verb.

Example: What are you looking forward to?
I am looking forward to going on holiday.
Or *I am looking forward to school breaking up for the summer.*

a What do you object to?
b What did you last apologise for?
c What do your parents insist on?
d What jobs at home are you responsible for?
e What did you dream about last night?
f What are you thinking of doing next year?
g What do you have difficulty doing?
h What would you be frightened of doing?
i What do you most enjoy doing?
j What do you consider a waste of time doing?
k What have your parents ever stopped you from doing?
l What do you enjoy taking part in?

5 Tell other students in the class about two or three of the most interesting things you learnt about your partner when asking each other the questions in the previous exercise.

Writing: Expanding and taking notes

When writing a composition using notes you have made from a lecture, a textbook or other reference materials, you need to be able to expand those notes clearly into a fuller written form.

It can also be useful to expand notes orally when you are giving a talk or a presentation of some kind. This is because it is usually much harder for listeners to understand a speaker who is simply reading out a previously written speech; listeners will follow a speaker who is talking from notes with much greater ease than one who is just reading the complete text.

1 First practise doing some oral expansion from notes. Read notes a, b and c and make sure that you understand what the note-taker meant by them. Imagine they are notes for three brief presentations you have to make.

In groups of three discuss what the notes on each of the subjects mean and how they would need to be expanded in a talk.

When you have discussed all three topics as a group, take one topic each and prepare to make a presentation on that topic.

a

> *Jamaica*
> Island in Caribbean, 160 km w Haiti and 14 km s Cuba
> Pop. (1989) 2,376,000
> Capital = Kingston
> Chief ethnic groups = African (76%); Afro-European (15%)
> Landscape = rugged mountains (Blue Mts over 2,000 m)
> Agri. = sugar, bananas, citrus fruits, coffee, cocoa, ginger, coconuts
> Inds. = bauxite (2nd largest producer in world), alumina, textiles, foodstuffs, rum, chemical products, tourism.

b

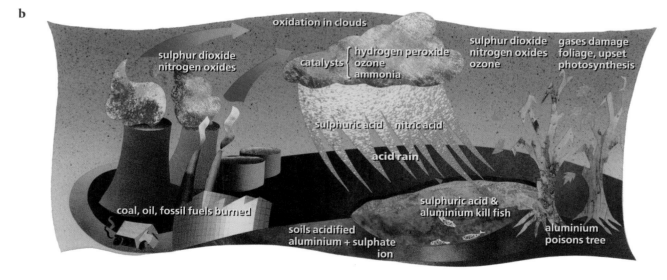

c

2 Now practise transforming notes into full written text. Expand the notes below into paragraphs of writing.

a

> Tonga (formerly Friendly Islands)
> Island group (169 islands, 36 inhab.) in sw Pacific, 2,250 km ne New Zealand
> Area = 646 sq km.
> Pop. (1989) 95,000 (98% = Tongans)
> Capital = Nuku'alofa
> Official lang. = Eng.
> Climate = semi-tropical. Ave. ann. temp. 23°C.
> 1899 British protectorate, under own monarchy; independence 1970
> Agri. = copra, coconuts, bananas, watermelons, yams, groundnuts, rice, maize, sugar cane, tobacco.
> Ind. (small but growing) = tourism, cottage handicrafts

b

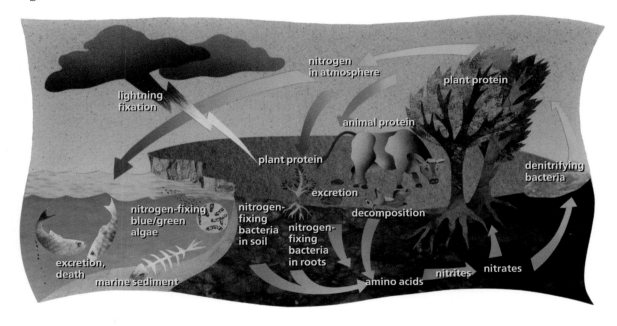

c

3 🔊 Listen to the lecture on the tape. It is in three parts. The notes on each part have been started in three different styles. Complete the notes for each part.

a

> *Basic facts about the brain*
> *Brain size =*
> *Men's brains*
> *Colour =*
> *Appearance =*
> *Surface area (i.e.   ) =*
> *Neurone =*
> *No. of neurones in brain =*
> *Role of neurones :*
>
> *This   (responsible for*
>
> *Frequency of chemical reactions =*

b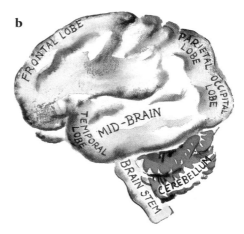

c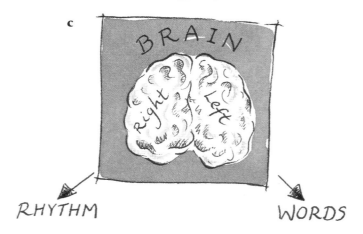

4 Which of the above three styles of taking notes do you prefer?

Do you have any techniques which you find particularly useful when taking notes? If so, share them with other students in the class.

5 Earlier in this unit, you looked at specialist vocabulary relating to the brain. Can you now add any more words and expressions to the lists you made in Vocabulary Exercise 1 on page 90?

6 Which of the lecturing techniques which you worked on in Listening Exercise 3 at the beginning of this unit were used in the lecture you have just listened to?

Speaking: Mini-lectures

Work with a partner.

1 Choose a subject that you are both interested in and plan a lecture on that subject.
2 Discuss which of the useful lecturing techniques considered in this unit you might use in your lecture.
3 Write your lecture out in note form, using whichever of the three note-taking methods from the previous exercise you prefer – or any other note-taking style.
4 Decide which of you is going to present each part of it.
5 Prepare any OHTs or other visuals needed for the lecture.
6 Give your lecture to other students in the class.
7 Take notes as you listen to each other's lectures.
8 Compare the notes taken during each lecture with those prepared by the lecturers prior to giving their talk.

The main aspects of language worked on in this unit are:	• reading law reports • difficult words to pronounce • relative clauses • commonly confused words • summarising

Warm-up: The law

1 Discuss in small groups.

a What films or TV dramas can you remember which featured a courtroom scene? What was the case about? What happened in the courtroom? What kind of people were the lawyers involved?

b In general, what kind of image of lawyers and courtrooms do you get from television and the cinema?

c Have you ever been present during a trial? If so, how did you feel?

d To what extent do TV and films present a realistic picture of lawyers and court scenes, in your opinion?

2 Before reading the first text, answer these questions about the law.

a What kind of work do lawyers do?

b In English law which of these is a solicitor and which is a barrister?
   – a lawyer who speaks in higher courts of law as defence or prosecution
   – a lawyer who gives legal advice and prepares legal documents and cases, occasionally appearing for his or her clients in lower courts of law

c Which role do you think is more prestigious and better-paid – that of a solicitor or that of a barrister? Why?

d Does being a lawyer attract you as a career? Which aspects of a lawyer's work appeal and which do not? Why?

e What do you know about an English courtroom? In what ways does it differ from a courtroom in your country?

f How do you think an English judge might justify why wigs are still worn in English courtrooms?

Reading: Legal decisions

1 Read the article *Solicitors to lose their case for wearing wigs* and complete the chart.

People mentioned in the article	Their opinions about solicitors wearing wigs in court	Where given, their reasons for those opinions
Lord Steyn		
SAHCA		
Lord Taylor		
the general public		
commercial court barristers		
Robert Owen, QC		
the Lord Chancellor		

Solicitors to lose their case for wearing wigs

The Lord Chancellor is expected to end the long and heated debate on wigs with a decision this month that solicitor-advocates must remain bareheaded.

The decision would infuriate the hundred or more solicitor-advocates, many of whom want the freedom to wear 18th-century horsehair in court. It would also contradict advice given to the Lord Chancellor, Lord Mackay of Clashfern, by his committee on the legal profession under Lord Steyn, the law lord.

Lord Steyn, in a letter to Lord Mackay before Christmas, said that if the justification for wigs was that they added dignity to court proceedings, that could not 'possibly justify a prohibition on solicitor-advocates wearing wigs in those very same court proceedings'. If the purpose of wigs was to underline the equality of advocates before the courts, then 'in the eyes of the court, all advocates ought to be treated as equal in every respect'.

Yesterday, Paul Hampton, chairman of the Solicitors' Association of Higher Court Advocates (SAHCA), which has made representations to the Lord Chancellor to be allowed to wear wigs, said, 'If this turns out to be the case it would be very disappointing.

'It would clearly be something we feel puts solicitor-advocates at a serious disadvantage (compared to barristers) because a number of people believe that the wearing of wigs in court confers a competitive advantage on the wearer.' Now that solicitors could obtain a certificate enabling them to take cases in the Crown Court and above, there would be some advocates with wigs and some without appearing before a bewigged judge, he said. 'The problem is that in the eyes of people in court, this is likely to show a close affinity between the wig-wearing advocate and the wig-wearing judge.'

Last July the Lord Chief Justice, Lord Taylor of Gosforth, issued a temporary practice direction on behalf of Lord Mackay, saying that solicitors should not be allowed to wear wigs pending further consideration. The order was witnessed after protests by barristers at seeing solicitors in Crown Courts wearing wigs.

The order stated Queen's Counsel were to wear a short wig and silk or stuff gown and junior counsel a short wig and stuff gown with bands. The debate began when Lord Taylor came to office in 1992 and shocked traditionalists by saying he would not mind removing wigs altogether. They looked 'slightly ridiculous', he said.

An 18-month consultation exercise followed and the overwhelming verdict from public and profession was that wigs should stay, despite support for them to go among barristers working in the commercial court.

The Bar conducted spot checks on the circuits to find out where wig-wearing solicitors had been seen. They found that the attitude of judges was inconsistent. In Birmingham and Lincoln, for example, wig-wearing solicitors were reported after being given permission by assistant recorders. On the North Eastern circuit, a 'sprinkling of solicitors' wearing wigs was reported but in Bradford, two judges had reportedly refused to allow wigs.

The Bar also took leading counsel's advice. Robert Owen, QC, said they were justified in opposing solicitors and stated that 'solicitors should not be allowed to pass themselves off as barristers'.

2 Before reading the second text, answer the following questions.

a The Sex Discrimination Act was introduced in Britain in 1975. What do you think the Act might state?

b Is there a similar Act in force in your country?

c Do such anti-discrimination acts solve all the problems they are intended to solve? Why (not)?

d What do the letters EEC stand for? What do you think an EEC Directive is?

e The word *precedent* is not used in the article but the concept of precedence is important for understanding the article. What does *precedent* mean and how is it used?

3 Now read the first part of the next article and complete the gaps. In each case one word is required.

No bias in dismissal through pregnancy illness

Brown v. Rentokil Ltd
Before Lord Allanbridge, Lord Murray and Lord Wylie
Judgement January 19th

Where a woman was dismissed because she was prevented from working by an illness arising out of her pregnancy, her dismissal was not direct sexual discrimination in terms of either the Sex Discrimination Act 1975 or EEC Directive 76/207.

An Extra Division of the Court of Session so held, (1) .... an appeal by Mrs Mary Brown against a decision of the Employment Appeal Tribunal of an application brought by her against Rentokil Ltd.

The Sex Discrimination Act 1975 provides 'A person discriminates against a woman in any circumstances relevant for the purposes of any provision of this Act if on the ground of her sex he treats her (2) .... favourably than he treats or would treat a man. A comparison of the cases of persons of different sex must be such that the relevant circumstances are the same, or not (3) .... different in the other.'

EEC Council Directive 76/207 provides '... with regard to conditions governing dismissal men and women are to be guaranteed the (4) .... conditions without discrimination on grounds of sex.'

Mr Colin McEachran, QC, for the appellant; Mr Nicholas Ellis for the respondents.

Lord Allanbridge, delivering the opinion of the court, said that the respondents had had a working rule, which had been a condition of the appellant's employment with them, that where an employee exceeded 26 weeks of continuous sick leave, that employee would be (5) .... That rule had been applied on at least one occasion in respect of a (6) .... employee.

The appellant had become pregnant and had not (7) .... from August 1990 until she was dismissed in February 1991. During that period she had submitted a series of medical certificates. The respondents (8) .... that her illness had been due to medical conditions arising out of her pregnancy.

The industrial tribunal had stated that the appellant had been treated in the same way as a male employee (9) .... through long term illness.

---

4 Now answer these questions about the situation you have just read about.

a Who are the two parties in the case and what are they disagreeing over?

b What was the argument used by each side?

c Whose side did the first court support?

5 Now read the next part of the text. Try to answer questions a to d before filling in the gaps.

a What case is referred to as precedent?
b What was the situation in that case?
c What was the judgement in that case and why?
d How does the Mary Brown case relate to the Webb case?

Now fill in the gaps in this part of the article.

In *Webb v. Emo Air Cargo (UK) Ltd* (1993) I WLR 49, Lord Keith of Kinkel had stated that there could be (10) .... doubt that in general to dismiss a woman because she was pregnant was unlawful direct discrimination (see James v. Eastleigh Borough Council [1990] 2 AC 751).

However, Lord Keith had said in Webb that the applicant had not been dismissed simply because she was pregnant, but because her pregnancy had the consequence that she would not be (11) .... for work at the critical time. He had gone on to explain that, but for her sex, Mrs Webb would not have been pregnant and but for her pregnancy she would not have been (12) ....

He had stated that if the 'but for' test applied to that situation, it had (13) .... to apply when the reason for the woman's being unavailable at the critical time was that she was then due to have an operation of a particularly gynaecological (14) ...., such as a hysterectomy.

But a man could be required to undergo an operation for some condition which was (15) .... to males, such as an abnormal prostate. Lord Keith had explained that the (16) .... comparison was not with any man but with a hypothetical man who would also be unavailable at the critical time. The relevant circumstance was expected unavailability. The precise (17) .... for the unavailability was not a relevant circumstance.

Their Lordships respectfully adopted and followed Lord Keith's reasoning. In the (18) .... case, it was not relevant that the precise reason for the appellant's illness was a condition, namely pregnancy, which was capable of affecting only women. No discrimination had arisen under the 1975 Act considered in isolation.

Their Lordships required, however, to take into account the answer of the European Court of Justice to the question referred by the House of Lords in *Webb* (1994) I IRLR 482. The appellant submitted that the answer, read along with the opinion of the advocate-general, clearly indicated that the 1976 Directive applied to the present case where a woman was dismissed due to an illness connected with pregnancy.

6 Read the next part of the article. Ignore the gaps and try to answer these questions.

a What was the second case of precedent referred to?
b What was the final decision with regard to Mary Brown?
c Why did the court decide in this way?

7 Now try to fill in the gaps in this last part of the article.

However, in *Handels-og v. Dansk Arbejdgierforing* (1992/ICR 332) the *Hertz* case, the European Court had said that 'the Directive does not envisage the case of an illness attributable to pregnancy or confinement ... In the case of an illness (19) .... itself after the maternity leave, there was no reason to distinguish an illness attributable to pregnancy or confinement from any other illness. Such a pathological condition was covered by the general rules applicable in the event of illness. Male and female workers are equally (20) .... to illness. Although certain disorders are, it is true, specific to one sex, the only question is whether a woman is dismissed on account of absence due to illness in the same circumstances as a man; if that is the case, then there is no direct discrimination on grounds of sex.' It would therefore appear that the appellant was not (21) .... by the Directive.

Webb did not distinguish the appellant's case from the *Hertz* case. *Webb* was not an 'illness' case, but a (22) .... case directly due to pregnancy.

In paragraph 25 (at p494) the European Court had stated: 'In the *Hertz* judgement ... the court drew a clear distinction between pregnancy and illness, even where the illness was attributable to pregnancy but manifests itself after the maternity leave ... there was (23) .... reason to distinguish such an illness from any other illness.'

That part of the ratio in *Hertz* applied to the present appeal. The appellant's absence having been due to illness and having been dismissed on account of that illness, she could not succeed on the relevant facts.

Mr McEachran argued that as *Hertz* had been dealing with an illness some time after (24) ...., the present appeal could be distinguished and he suggested that, if the court had any (25) ...., it should refer the case to the European Court.

Their Lordships had reached the conclusion that the present case was reasonably clear and free from doubt in view of the European Court's decision in *Hertz*.

8 This article is a full law report. It was written for those with a professional interest in the law. How is this clear from the content of the article?

9 Follow these instructions and do some more work on the vocabulary of the two articles.

1 Choose the article that interests you more. Underline any words or expressions in that text that you do not understand or are not sure whether you understand properly.
2 Work with two other students who chose the same text. Tell each other which words and expressions you underlined. If a student in the group knows a word or expression underlined by others, then he or she should explain it for them.
3 Share out any remaining words and expressions which no one is sure about and look them up in an English-English dictionary.
4 Explain the words or expressions you looked up to the other students in your group.
5 Prepare ten vocabulary test questions for another group of students which chose the same text. You could ask, for example, either:
   What do you call the false hair which an English judge wears?
   or:
   What does the word *wig* mean?
   or you could ask the students to fill gaps in a sentence, e.g.
   Solicitors would like to have the right to wear a .... *in court.*
6 Get together with another group of students which worked on the same text. Test each other with the sets of questions which you prepared.

Listening: Legal decisions

🔲 Lindsay Davies is a woman barrister. You are going to listen to her answers to these questions. Before listening, predict how you think she might answer the questions. Make notes on what her answers were and then compare your notes with those made by another student.

a How unusual is it to be a female barrister in England?

b What do you enjoy and what do you not enjoy about your work?

c Do you think that solicitors should be allowed to wear wigs in court?

d Do you think that decisions in cases like Mary Brown's might be different if more judges and law-makers were women?

e Do you think that male and female barristers are always treated equally?

Speaking: Difficult words to pronounce

1 A number of words connected with the law can be difficult to pronounce. Check that you know what each of the following words and expressions mean.

> law lawyer
> law-abiding lawful
> unlawful lawless
> legislature judge
> judgement jury
> juror magistrate
> manslaughter murder
> murderer gaol
> to convict a convict
> regina perjury
> sub judice beneficiary
> to bequeath heir
> heiress to inherit
> a police constable
> a lieutenant
> a police sergeant
> deceive deceit
> an affidavit

2 🔲 Repeat the words in Exercise 1 after the speaker on the tape.

3 Make up sentences using as many as possible of the words in Exercise 1 in each sentence. Give your sentences to other students for them to practise reading aloud.

4 Choose one of the two legal texts from the beginning of the unit. You are going to practise reading it aloud. Follow these instructions.

1 Choose one section to work on.

2 Underline the key words in the article, in other words the words which carry the main meaning of the text – for example, the underlined words in the sentence below rather than grammar words like articles, auxiliary verbs and prepositions.
The <u>Lord Chancellor</u> is <u>expected</u> to <u>end</u> the <u>long</u> and <u>heated debate</u> on <u>wigs</u> with a <u>decision</u> this <u>month</u> that <u>solicitor advocates</u> must <u>remain bareheaded</u>.

3 How will the pronunciation of the underlined words differ from the pronunciation of the words which are not underlined?

4 Read one or two sentences from the section of text which you have been working on aloud to the rest of the class.

5 Listen very carefully to each other's pronunciation, paying particular attention to the pronunciation of the key words.

6 Discuss with the teacher any such words which you feel that you or other students in the class may not be pronouncing correctly.

Vocabulary: Easily confused words

It is particularly important for lawyers to use the right word at the right time as words that seem similar can convey significantly different meanings.

1 Explain the difference between the following pairs (or sets) of sentences from different law court situations. Use a dictionary or other reference book, if necessary.

a The vase that was stolen was priceless.
   The vase that was stolen was worthless.
b The witness said the attacker was a stranger.
   The witness said the attacker was a foreigner.
c The child was always very willing.
   The child was always very wilful.
d His behaviour was inhuman.
   His behaviour was inhumane.
e The police have carried out exhausting interviews with the main suspects.
   The police have carried out exhaustive interviews with the main suspects.
f The defendant always seemed to behave in a very carefree way.
   The defendant always seemed to behave in a very careless way.
g Mr Brown spoke very shortly to me.
   Mr Brown spoke very briefly to me.
h He is a large man.
   He is a great man.
i Her husband was a heavy man.
   Her husband was a hard man.
   Her husband was a difficult man.
j The brother he had told us he lived with turned out to be imaginary.
   The brother he had told us he lived with turned out to be imaginative.

2 Explain the difference in meaning between the words in the groups below. Use a dictionary to help you if necessary.

a male/masculine
b verdict/sentence
c valueless/invaluable
d surely/certainly
e sensitive/sensible
f satisfying/satisfactory
g memories/memoirs/souvenirs
h lone/lonely/alone
i imagination/fantasy
j distinctive/distinct/distinguished
k boundary/border/frontier
l unlawful/lawless

3 Now write sentences which clearly illustrate the difference in meaning between the words in the previous exercise.

Grammar: Relative clauses

1 Look at these examples of relative clauses from the texts and answer the questions about them.

The decision would infuriate the hundred or more solicitor-advocates, many of whom want the freedom to wear 18th-century horsehair in court.

a Is it correct to say *many of who*?
b What is the difference between *the woman who I work with* and *the woman with whom I work*?
c How much do you think *whom* is used in contemporary English?
d Compare the following example from the text (1) with this – also correct – version (2):

(1) *Yesterday Paul Hampton, chairman of SAHCA, which has made representations to the Lord Chancellor to be allowed to wear wigs, said …*
(2) *Yesterday Paul Hampton, chairman of SAHCA, who have made representations to the Lord Chancellor to be allowed to wear wigs, said …*

e What two differences are there between these two sentences? How would you account for these differences?
f Can you suggest any nouns apart from *association* which lead to similar examples.
g What has happened to the relative clause in each of the examples below?

The decision would contradict advice given to the Lord Chancellor by his committee on the legal profession.
Lord Allanbridge, delivering the opinion of the court, said that the respondents had a working rule …
It would clearly be something we feel puts solicitor-advocates at a serious disadvantage.

h When is it possible to omit the relative pronoun in this way?
i Which relative pronoun is being used in the following sentence? Why is this possible?

The 1976 Directive clearly applied to the present case where a woman was dismissed due to an illness connected with pregnancy.

j Suggest five other nouns that *where* might follow in the role of a relative pronoun.
k *When* can similarly sometimes be used as a relative pronoun. Give five nouns which it might follow.
l *Why* is used as a relative pronoun after one word only – what is that word?

2 Now look at some more examples of relative clauses and answer the questions about them.

I could not understand what the lawyer was saying.
I could not understand all that the lawyer was saying.

a Are *what* and *that* interchangeable in these two sentences?
b When is *what* used as a relative pronoun?
c When is *that* used as a relative pronoun?

The witness spoke very softly, which made it difficult to hear him.

d What is *which* referring to in the example above?
e What do you notice about the punctuation of this example?

That is the woman whose employers sacked her when they discovered she was pregnant.
It was a case whose subtleties were too complex for me to follow.

f Can *whose* be used to refer back to both people and things?
g If the speaker wanted to avoid *whose* in the second example above, what could he or she say?

3 Are the sentences below correct? If not, correct the errors.

a I couldn't see everything what was happening at the front of the courtroom.
b The trial didn't last very long which was a relief to us all.
c It was difficult to hear all what the defendant said.
d The police took a lot of photos at the scene of the crime, some of them were used as evidence in court.
e A jogger found the body which the detectives had been looking for it for a week.
f Can you recommend me a firm which I could find a good lawyer?
g Some people in Britain are in favour of bringing back capital punishment, which was done away with in the 1960s.
h He murdered his wife that he had married only six months previously.
i The lawyers' fee was enormous, what came as a great shock to us.
j It is impossible to understand the reason which he committed such a crime.

It was all Greek to me

4 Join each of the pairs of sentences to make one sentence, using a relative clause.

a I read those law reports. Several of them were very interesting.
b I once heard Lord Hangham give a speech. He was arguing very forcibly for the reinstatement of capital punishment.
c The Greek policeman spoke to me. I didn't understand anything.
d The highjacking was a very frightening experience. I've never had a more frightening one.
e That is the spot. I was mugged on that spot.
f Have you ever met the girl? Her sports car was found at the scene of the crime.
g We didn't know if the criminals would be caught. That was very alarming.
h That is the woman. I saw that woman when she was opening the safe with a key.

Study skills: Summarising

1 Answer these questions about summary writing.

a What is a summary?
b What sorts of things from an original text would you include in a summary and what sorts of things would you not include?
c When might you need to write a summary in 'real life'?
d Why is writing a summary of an English text a useful thing to do from a language learning point of view?

In general, writing a summary or precis is a matter of concentrating on what is essential in what the writer is saying and then leaving out all unnecessary detail.

It can be a useful focusing exercise to summarise any text you have read very briefly – in just one sentence, if this is possible. This helps you to think in a very precise way about what a text is trying to say.

2 Write a sentence summarising each of the two articles you have been studying in this unit. Compare your sentences with those written by other students.

Having thought about the overall meaning of the text, it is now necessary to go back and think about the different parts of the text which fed into the summary sentence you wrote.

If a text is well written, then each paragraph will have something distinctive to add to the piece of writing and so it is a good idea to work through the text summarising each paragraph in one sentence. Where paragraphs are very short – as is typical of newspaper articles – then it may be appropriate to cover two or more paragraphs in one summary sentence.

Conversely, if you are working with a more academic text with very long paragraphs, you may find it necessary to use more than one sentence when summarising each paragraph.

3 Look at the article *Solicitors to lose their case for wearing wigs* and follow these instructions.

1 A number of the paragraphs here are already only one sentence. How could you group the paragraphs so that the ideas which each group of paragraphs is presenting can be conveyed in just one summarising sentence?
2 Write a sentence for each of the sets of paragraphs you grouped together.

It is now necessary to combine the set of individual sentences based on a paragraph or group of paragraphs to make one connected paragraph, summarising the whole of the original text. It may well be appropriate to begin or end this paragraph with the initial sentence which you wrote to sum up the text as a whole.

4 Combine the sentences you wrote about the article on wigs in Exercises 2 and 3 in order to make a well-connected paragraph summarising the whole article.

Compare your summary paragraph with that written by one or more other students. Make any changes you feel would be appropriate after looking at other students' work.

5 Write a summary of the article *No bias in dismissal through pregnancy illness.*

Speaking: Legal articles

1 As homework, find an article from a newspaper or magazine on the subject of a legal case, a crime or an issue relating to the law that is currently in the news. You may choose an article that is not in English, but you must be prepared to summarise it orally and discuss it in English.

Prepare to tell the other students in the class:

a what the article is about – in other words, you need to summarise the article orally in an effective way;
b why you find it interesting.

You may also like to prepare some questions to ask the other students in order to find out their opinions on the subject of your article.

2 Follow the instructions below and share your articles with each other.

1 Work in groups of three or four students, telling each other about the articles you chose.
2 When you have fully discussed each of your articles, choose the most interesting one to present to the class as a whole. The student who brought the article to class should summarise its contents for the rest of the class, but other students in the group should explain why they found it particularly interesting to discuss.
3 As a class, discuss the most interesting articles from each of the small groups.

The main aspects of language worked on in this unit are:
- understanding drama
- speaking – expressing emotion
- features of spoken grammar
- colours and their associations
- watching films and drama

Warm-up: Drama

Look at the pictures and answer the questions.

a Describe what you can see.
b From the clues in the pictures, what do you think the drama might be about?
c The drama makes considerable use of the technique of flashbacks. What do you understand by this term?

Listening: The Eyes of Max Carrados

1 📼 You are going to listen to part of a story in a series called *The Eyes of Max Carrados*. Max Carrados is an extremely clever detective, in the Sherlock Holmes tradition. He is also blind. This play opens with a visit he receives from Madeleine Whitmarsh. She explains the difficult situation she is in.

Listen to the first two scenes of the play and answer the questions which your teacher asks you after each scene.

2 🔊 Now listen to the next part of the scene at the reading of the will and fill in the gaps.

LAWYER: Is there (1) .... difficulty?

WILLIAM: None in the (2) .... I get all the (3) .... farmland. Brother Frank gets the (4) .... and the scrubs. No difficulty there.

FRANK: Damn the man. Damn you too. Well, let's see if you're still (5) .... this time next year.

WILLIAM: What do you (6) ....?

FRANK: Let's see how your precious farmlands (7) .... when they're next door to my mines and my (8) ....

WILLIAM: You're going to (9) .... the land?

FRANK: Those coalseams are (10) .... ten times your wheatfields, brother.

WILLIAM: You can't do it.

FRANK: You can't stop me.

LAWYER: Yes, he can.

FRANK: What?

LAWYER: Yes, he can.

WILLIAM: I thought you'd (11) .... Yes. How can I stop him?

LAWYER: This is your (12) .... father's final stipulation. Neither of you may do anything to exploit his (13) .... of the lands either for minerals or development without the full and (14) .... consent of the other. He can stop you with a (15) .... word.

WILLIAM: (16) ....!

3 🔊 Now listen to the last scenes from the play and answer the questions which your teacher asks you.

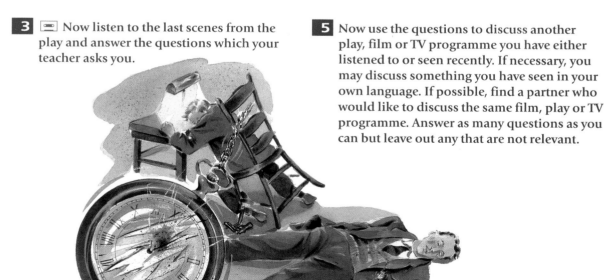

4 Listening to a play in English on the radio or watching one on TV, at the theatre or in the cinema is a very useful way of extending your English. You can help yourself to make the most of this experience by writing something about the play afterwards. Below are some questions which are appropriate for any play you may hear or see.

Answer as many questions as you can about the play you have just listened to.

a What is the play called and who wrote it?

b Why does the play have this name?

c When and where is the play set?

d How many characters are there in the play?

e How would you describe each of the main characters?

f Summarise the plot of the play.

g How does the main character / do the main characters change in the course of the play?

h What are the main emotions experienced in the course of the play?

i Could the play have taken place in a different setting and a different period without too many changes?

j What do you think was the writer's main intention in writing this play?

k How would you comment on the actors' performance in the play?

l Write down five words or expressions which you learnt from the play or heard used in an interesting way in the play.

m Would you recommend this play to someone else? Why (not)?

5 Now use the questions to discuss another play, film or TV programme you have either listened to or seen recently. If necessary, you may discuss something you have seen in your own language. If possible, find a partner who would like to discuss the same film, play or TV programme. Answer as many questions as you can but leave out any that are not relevant.

Speaking: Expressing emotion

1 Look at the list of emotions and follow the instructions below.

1 Check that you understand what each of the emotions below mean. When have you felt – or might you feel – such an emotion?

2 Organise the emotions into any categories that seem appropriate to you.

> anger   suspicion   delight   fear   disgust   pride   panic
> amusement   relief   dislike   anxiety   admiration
> astonishment   annoyance   curiosity

2 Practise saying each of the following in a number of different ways expressing each of the emotions named underneath.

a *It's finally over, isn't it?*
anger
suspicion
delight
fear
disgust

b *You want me to marry you.*
pride
panic
amusement
relief
dislike

c *Miss Whitmarsh.*
anxiety
admiration
astonishment
annoyance
curiosity

d *Yes.*
All fifteen emotions.

3 What did you notice about what happened to your voice when you were expressing different emotions?

4 📼 Read the tapescript on page 171 as you listen again to the extracts from the play. Note down beside the script the emotions from the list in Exercise 1 that are expressed or suggested by the lines.

5 In small groups practise reading the script aloud. Express the emotions that you noted down in as extreme a way as possible.

6 Choose one of these sentences from the text.

– I really don't know where to start.
– He promised it to me.
– You can't do it.
– I can still see his face.
– Who'd have thought it?

Say the sentences in one of the fifteen emotions you have been practising. Can the rest of the class guess the emotion you are trying to express?

Vocabulary: Colours and their associations

1 It could be said that Miss Whitmarsh arrived on Max Carrados's doorstep *out of the blue*. What does this expression mean?

Can you think of any other examples of English expressions based on colours?

2 Rewrite the sentences in a way that explains the colour expression underlined.

a The black economy is very important in a number of countries.
b Tomorrow is a red-letter day for me.
c He can talk until he is blue in the face but it won't make any difference.
d Jane painted a very black picture of the situation.
e Kay's been feeling pretty browned off for some time.
f The thief was caught red-handed.
g The grass is greener on the other side of the fence.
h I just can't be doing with red tape.
i That new office block has become a bit of a white elephant.
j That part of town is the red-light district.
k Brian doesn't have much grey matter, I'm afraid.
l That argument is a red herring.
m It makes me see red when he talks like that.
n I'm afraid you're in the red again.

3 What is meant by the use of each of the colours in the sentences below?

a Jim's a true blue but his wife definitely has pinkish tendencies.
b Don't be so yellow.
c A lot of green issues are in the news at the moment.
d I wish he wouldn't tell so many blue jokes.
e Bill has got two black eyes.
f That's a bit of a grey area.
g What a golden opportunity!
h Her novel is full of purple passages.
i Why do you feel so blue?
j He made me quite green with his stories of his holiday.
k Is it wrong to tell a white lie?
l Some people disapprove of his black humour.
m He's still green – you must expect him to make mistakes.
n A lot of the passengers looked distinctly green.

4 Do the colours used in the sentences in the previous two exercises have the same meanings in your language?

What associations do the colours blue, red, green, yellow, white and black have in your language?

Grammar: Features of spoken grammar

The features of spoken English which you are going to look at in this section are:

– ellipsis
– subject noun phrases
– past perfect for giving explanations
– characteristic phrases

One of the main features of spoken English is the frequent use of ellipsis, i.e. when we speak we often leave out words or phrases which can be clearly understood from the context.

Look at this exchange:

MADELEINE: Father, why did you hate him so much? He was your brother!
WILLIAM: Half-brother.

Half-brother is elliptical. What we understand is *He was my half-brother*.

1 Find examples of ellipsis in the extracts from the tapescript below. Add in the words which have been omitted through the use of ellipsis.

a – What's so funny?
   – Everything. Pa's idea of equality wasn't exactly the same as yours.
b – Those coalseams are worth ten times your wheatfields, brother.
   – You can't do it.
   – You can't stop me.
   – Yes, he can.
   – What?
   – Yes, he can.
   – I thought you'd finished. How can I stop him?
c – Uncle William.
   – Have you inherited your father's stupidity? No, never, not while I'm alive.
d – Two things were immediately apparent as you walked into this room. You're dressed in mourning and you're carrying a newspaper. I assume that it has something to do with this business.
   – Yes, yes, it does.
   – May I have it please?
   – But surely?
   – If you please.
   – Of course. Here.
e – No, I'm all right.
   – All right? Look, there's no blood. Your father must have missed him.
   – No, I felt the shot.
   – Then how in the world?
   – I don't know. Oh, surely not.

2 🔊 Using ellipsis will make your English sound much more natural. Listen to the pairs of examples on the tape. In each case, which version do you prefer? Why?

Another common feature of spoken grammar is the use of an extended noun clause at the beginning of a sentence to introduce the subject the speaker is going to talk about. For example,

That nephew of yours walked in here … .

In ordinary conversation we often do this at greater length and in a looser way than is usually done in drama or any other scripted version of spoken English. We say things like:

That girl in the top class with the very short black hair is moving into the flat next door to mine.
The bike I was telling you about yesterday, the one that Mike's selling, I think I might try it out this evening.
That film at the Odeon Jane recommended that has had all those awful reviews – do you fancy going to see it tonight?
The lady who works in the corner shop – her husband, his sister owns the shop.

3 Write some examples of your own to introduce the underlined words in the sentences below. Try to elaborate on the noun in a full and interesting way.

a That family has bought a new car.
b I met him last night.
c Silvia gave it to me as a birthday present.
d It is for sale.
e That teacher is supposed to be very good.

Work in groups of three. Read out your sentences to each other and choose the most interesting example of each to read out to the class as a whole.

4 An analysis of spoken English shows that the most common use of the past perfect tense is to give an explanation for something that happened. You have an example at the beginning of the extract from the Max Carrados story.

MAX CARRADOS: Why did you come to me, Miss Whitmarsh?
MISS WHITMARSH: I'd heard of your wonderful powers.

Write a sentence to explain the following situations, using the past perfect tense. The first one has been done for you as an example.

a William was very pleased with the way the estate was divided. *He had been left all the good land.*
b Frank was very unhappy with the way the estate was divided.
c Miss Whitmarsh's father was slumped across the desk.
d William hated his nephew, Frank.
e The bullet did not kill Frank.

5 Now continue the following sentences using a past perfect tense.

a He didn't get here on time because …
b The meeting was postponed as …
c She agreed to marry him since …
d The company went bankrupt. The reason was that …
e Their financial difficulties were caused by the fact that …
f Jill overslept because …

6 It is useful to listen to and read drama because it can be a rich source of phrases common in spoken English – even if the characters in a play are often more articulate than most native speakers are most of the time!

Look at the tapescript of the extract from the drama on page 171 and write down six phrases or sentences which:

a you find characteristic of spoken as opposed to written English and

b you feel you might find useful when speaking English yourself.

You might choose, for instance, *does it matter* or *not that you've anything to wait for*.

Compare your choice of phrases or sentences with those selected by another student.

7 Work with the student whose selection you looked at in the previous exercise. Write a dialogue together in which you make use of as many of the phrases or sentences you selected as possible.

Speaking: Drama

1 Work in groups of three or four. You are going to prepare a short play. Follow these instructions.

1 Choose one of these situations as the basis for your play – a crime, a proposal of marriage, making or reading a will.

2 Choose three emotions from this list to include in your play:

admiration	disgust
amusement	dislike
anger	excitement
annoyance	love
anxiety	pride
astonishment	relief
curiosity	suspicion
delight	terror

3 Decide on the characters and the plot for your play.

4 Choose a title for your play. If possible, the title should include a colour used with either a literal or a metaphorical meaning.

5 Consider how you might be able to make use of some of the elements of the grammar of spoken English which you have worked on in this unit.

6 Discuss how you are going to perform your play to the other students in the class.

7 Rehearse your play.

8 Perform it to the other students in the class.

9 As you watch plays by other students in your class, think about which emotions are being expressed in those plays. How well are those emotions conveyed?

The main aspects of language worked on in this unit are:	• reading newspapers • punctuation • prepositions • the language of newspapers • skimming and scanning

Warm-up: Newspapers

Discuss with two or three other students whether you agree with these statements. Modify the statements if you want. Be prepared to justify your opinions.

a Reading newspapers is a waste of time – it's better to read a good novel.

b Newspapers prevent a lot of crime.

c It is every citizen's responsibility to read a newspaper regularly.

d Newspapers shouldn't print stories about famous people's private lives.

e Newspapers should print more good news.

f It's better to learn the news from TV or radio than from newspapers.

g Newspapers distort people's view of the world.

h People own newspapers because they want to educate and inform the world.

Reading: Newspaper stories

1 Here is the same news story as told by two different newspapers. Work with a partner. Each read one of the stories and then tell each other about what you have read.

£1,000 for boy held at police station

A BOY has been awarded £1,000 damages for being falsely imprisoned by police when he was three years old.

Levi Gallagher spent four hours in a juvenile detention room after his father was ejected from a train for offensive behaviour during a trip to the seaside.

Yesterday a jury at Liverpool County Court decided that the police should have made special arrangements for Levi, who is now five.

His father Mr Marcus Gallagher, 26, said later: 'He kept crying and wanting to go home and he wasn't even offered a drink of water or anything to eat. It was a boiling hot day but when I asked if we could leave the door open, I was told that they weren't there to look after children.

'For a long time afterwards he was petrified whenever he saw a police-man. He got really upset when I took him to watch Liverpool play and he saw all the police there. I had to reassure him that they were not going to lock him up.'

Mr Gallagher of Toxteth, Liverpool, told the court he had to remain at the station overnight because of outstanding fine warrants. But a custody sergeant ignored his request to ask relatives to collect Levi.

Officers claimed that Mr Gallagher had been uncooperative and only offered information when it was suggested that social workers might become involved.

Meanwhile, police were ordered to pay costs as well as the £1,000, which Levi will not receive until he is 18. Until then, it will remain with the court, accruing interest at two per cent.

£1,000 PAY-OUT TO TOT, 5, KEPT IN NICK

POLICE must pay £1,000 damages for false imprisonment to a boy aged **FIVE**.

Levi Gallagher was held for four hours after his dad was nicked for smoking on a train.

But yesterday a jury decided the law had been heavy-handed with him; they ordered the award to be paid into court now – and kept as a nest-egg for Levi when he's 18.

Levi and his dad Marcus, 26, were hauled off to the nick in August 1992 when transport police caught Marcus having a cigarette on a train while on a day out to Southport.

But at the cop shop it was discovered that there was a warrant for outstanding fines against him and he was told he was being banged up overnight.

Ignored

A county court hearing at Liverpool heard that Levi was kept in a custody room and it was four hours before desk sergeants made any efforts to contact relatives to pick him up.

But Merseyside police claimed Marcus had been uncooperative and only came up with names when he was threatened with Social Services.

After yesterday's award, Marcus, of Toxteth Liverpool, insisted the boy had been ignored by the cops.

He said, 'Levi had been really looking forward to the day and was totally distraught when we were kept for all that time in a juvenile detention room.

'He kept crying and wanting to go home and wasn't even offered a drink of water or anything to eat.

'It was a boiling hot day but when I asked if we could have the door open, I was told that they weren't there to look after children. They should make children their priority.'

Mr Gallagher, a single parent of Toxteth, Liverpool, was later fined £12 for smoking on a train.

2 Now read both stories again. With a partner list all the differences you can find between the content and style of the two stories. For example, the first story just says that the boy's father was 'ejected from a train for offensive behaviour' whereas the second story specifies that he was smoking; the second story has a much bigger headline than the first.

Vocabulary: The language of tabloid newspapers

1 You noticed that the language used in the second story differed from that used in the first one. Here are some of the words and expressions characteristic of tabloid newspapers from the second story. What are the more neutral equivalents in each case? (They can often, though not always, be found in the other version of the story.)

a pay-out
b a tot
c the nick
d to be nicked
e the law
f cop shop
g hauled off
h banged up
i to pick up
j boiling hot

2 🖭 Here are some more sentences from popular newspapers using expressions typically found in tabloids. You are going to listen to the headlines from some newspapers on tape. Match each headline with its story below.

'Translate' each of the sentences below into neutral English.

a The company – whose slogan is It's Good to Talk – booted out trainee Karen Hawkes, 33, when it was discovered she was taking time to chat to people ringing up directory enquiries.

b ALTHOUGH he was once tipped as a future Cabinet Minister, David Mellor has shown himself in his true colours as a serial sleazebag.

c BEEB chiefs were celebrating last night after its Monday-night soap knocked ITV's most popular soap off the top ratings spot for the first time ever.

d PETITE soccer star's missus, blonde Debbie, 33, was too stunned to speak when we broke the news yesterday of how her husband fixed matches for money.

e TWO MEN were being quizzed by police after a swoop at Woolies last night following an anonymous tip-off.

f A PRISONER has gone on hunger strike after repeatedly being dished up greens. His sister says he just can't abide them but the screws say he's just stirring up trouble.

3 The language of headlines in popular newspapers is also characteristic. Look at these headlines and answer these questions.

a What do you notice about their grammar?
b What do you notice about their vocabulary?
c What do you think each story will be about?

List all the words in the headlines which seem to be typical of newspaper headlines rather than ordinary English. Write the equivalent in normal English beside each word.

Di double steals show at big book launch

MoD under fire as sacked service girls share £1½ m

BOMB PLOTTER JAILED

Ice crash crew saved by salami

PM targets White House

MP's son in US race row

Teddies foil baby kidnaps

Spider smuggler jailed

Cabinet stalemate on £5bn cutbacks

BRITON RELIVES BACKPACK ORDEAL

4 You are going to write some eye-catching newspaper headlines.

1 With a partner write two or three headlines that you think would be sure to catch the attention of the students in your class.
2 Compare the headlines you wrote with those written by other pairs.

Writing: Punctuation

Although English is freer than many languages are about the use of punctuation marks, it is still important to use them appropriately. Failure to do so makes your writing much harder to understand and may indeed result in your giving the wrong impression.

1 You are going to practise putting punctuation into a newspaper article. Draw each of these punctuation marks.

apostrophe   asterisk
brackets   colon   comma
dash   exclamation mark
full stop   hyphen
inverted commas
question mark   semi-colon

2 Now revise your knowledge of the rules of punctuation by completing the blanks in the rules governing three of the less usual punctuation marks below.

a An .... is used to show that letters have been missed out in a contracted form, e.g. ....

b It is also used before or after s to indicate possession. It is used before the s .... and after the s when ....

c It can also be used to make a plural form with words that do not normally have a plural form, e.g. *if* and *why* as in the sentence
....

d It can, similarly, be used to make the plural of letters, e.g.
.... or, sometimes, numbers, e.g. ....

e The .... is particularly common in informal writing. It is often used to introduce an afterthought or something that is unexpected or surprising or simply to add in an extra idea. In more formal writing the extra idea might be put in .... rather than between ....

f .... are used when we are quoting what someone says.

g They can also be used around titles of books or films as in the sentence ....

h They are also used when we want to highlight the fact that we are giving a word or expression a special meaning, as in the sentence
....

3 Capital letters are another important element of punctuation.
Complete this chart which summarises how we use them.

When used	Example	Another example
First letter of sentence	We met at eight.	
	George Washington	
	Monday	
	July	
	the Managing Director, Professor Macdonald	
	Atlantic Ocean, Rocky Mountains	
	France, North Carolina	
	Spanish, Swiss	
	Gone with the Wind, The Financial Times	
	Sikh, Jewish	

4 Now practise using a whole range of punctuation marks by writing the newspaper article opposite with all the necessary marks and capital letters. In this article two different TV stars are asked to describe their most embarrassing moments.

my worst moment

jeremy paxman tv interviewer i well recall being sent out as a young reporter to cover an industrial dispute in belfast i found the trade union representative set up the camera and on the signal asked him the first question mr kennedy whats behind this dispute thinking he hadnt heard me i said again mr kennedy whats this dispute about silence again i concluded that he was deaf so i shouted at him mr kennedy what on earths this dispute about finally a response the only dispute here is that my names johnson not kennedy

dr patrick moore obe astronomer way back around 1959 i was presenting a live television programme about astronomy i opened my mouth to make some worldshattering pronouncement and in flew a large fly what to do to my eternal credit i swallowed it the producer said afterwards that he saw a look of glazed horror come into my eyes then i gave a strangled gulp and went on my mother put it well yes dear she said thoughtfully nasty for you but so much worse for the fly i suppose it was

5 Write out your own most embarrassing experience without any punctuation or capital letters. Exchange stories with a partner and write out each other's work with punctuation. If you think there are any errors in what your partner has written, discuss these with your partner and, if appropriate, write an improved version in your punctuated text.

Grammar: Prepositions

1 Twenty prepositions have been missed out of the newspaper article below. Can you put them back in? (The headline is correct.)

War of the rose lands gardener in court for border attack

AN OVER-KEEN GARDENER appeared court yesterday accused throttling his neighbour a dispute his beloved pink rose.

The row Wilf Dobb and his neighbour 30 years, Rita Griffiths, arose because a rose. Mr Dobb tied it string the boundary fence their gardens, thinking it belonged him.

But Mrs Griffiths, Sarn Lane, Caergwyrlie, Clwyd, knew the fence was hers and repeatedly snipped the string after Mr Dobb kept retying it, magistrates Mold, Clwyd, were told. So Mr Dobb turned a 150-foot rope, half an inch thick.

Mrs Griffiths told the court that as she started to cut the rope a pair of scissors, 'he wrapped it my neck and pulled it tight. I thought I was going to die.'

Mr Dobb was convicted assault and given a two-year conditional discharge £120 costs plus £75 compensation Mrs Griffiths.

She said afterwards she was pleased the verdict but added, 'It's me who has to serve the sentence. It's left me tranquilisers and we may have to move home even though we own our house and he only rents.' Mr Dobb would only say, 'I'm not a nice person.'

The rose has died.

2 ▭ Listen to the news article read on tape and check your answers to Exercise 1.

Study skills: Skimming and scanning

Skimming means looking at a piece of text quickly in order to get a quick impression of what it is about. Scanning is looking over a piece of text quickly in order to find one particular piece of information you are looking for. Skimming can be useful, for example, if you are trying to decide whether to buy a book and scanning is what you do when you look at a local newspaper to find out what is on at your nearest cinema.

It can be useful to practise the skills of skimming and scanning in English as, for many people, it takes confidence not to feel you have to read every word in a foreign language in order to be sure that you know what the text is about.

This exercise practises both skimming and scanning. Try the exercise as a competition – which group can write down the correct answers to all the questions first?

For the exercise, each group needs a copy of the same newspaper.

What is the name of the newspaper and what date is it?	
How many pictures are there on the front page? Who or what do they show?	
How many different stories are there on the front page? What is the main topic of each one?	
Look at the TV guide. Are there any films on tonight?	
What would you most like to watch on TV tonight? When is it on?	
Look at the entertainments listings in the paper. What kinds of entertainments are listed? Which city (cities) are they on in?	
What is your favourite spectator sport? Is there anything about that sport in the paper?	
Look at the whole newspaper. What countries can you find articles about? List them.	
What was the weather like yesterday in (a) London, (b) New York and (c) the capital of your country?	
What was the exchange rate for your country's currency?	
What are the editorials about? Write a sentence about each editorial summarising the topic and the opinion presented.	

Writing: Stories

You and your class are going to produce a collection of short stories, inspired by short newspaper articles. Follow these instructions.

1 Your teacher will give you a short newspaper article to use as inspiration for a story. Alternatively, you may choose an article from the newspaper you studied in the previous section. You should use the newspaper article merely as a starting-point and may add or change details as much as you wish.

2 In groups of three or four, take turns to describe the newspaper article you have been given or have chosen. In each case, discuss with the other students:
   – How might this situation have developed?
   – Where exactly did the situation take place?
   – What were the people involved like?
   – How did they feel?
   – What might happen next?
Spend about five minutes discussing each of the stories.

3 Now, individually, write your story, thinking carefully about how to bring it alive and make it interesting for the reader. Some techniques which you worked on in Unit 10 and which you might like to use are:
   – using direct speech
   – appealing to the reader's five senses (i.e. referring to sounds and smells, for example)
   – referring to the characters' feelings
   – using a variety of tenses (in an appropriate way!)

The main aspects of language worked on in this unit are:

- understanding jokes
- telling jokes
- word order
- puns

Warm-up: Jokes

1 Look at the cartoons below. Are they funny? Why? Why not?

> Did you hear about the staff nurse on the surgical ward who was known as Appendix? All the surgeons took her out.

> What do you think he is thinking about?

> I imagine he's wondering where he left his clothes.

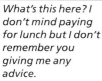

> What's this here? I don't mind paying for lunch but I don't remember you giving me any advice.

> Don't you remember? You asked me what I recommended and I said 'Try the Boeuf Bourguignon'.

> I think I'd like a little game.

> Draughts or chess, sir?

2 Would these cartoons translate effectively into your language? Why? Why not?

3 Discuss these questions with some other students.

a Are there are any subjects which are often used as the subject of jokes in your language – politicians, mothers-in-law, elephants or people from particular towns, for instance?

b And do jokes take any typical forms in your language – questions and answers, shaggy dog tales, for instance?

c Jokes often relate to subjects that are embarrassing in some way. They can also be based on the belittling of another group of people – women or people of a different nationality, for instance. How do you feel about jokes of these types?

d What sorts of jokes do you enjoy?

e Are there any sorts of jokes that you object to?

Listening: Jokes

1 There are a number of typical formats for jokes in English. These include:

– Jokes that begin: *What's the difference between …*
– Jokes that begin: *What do you call …*
– Jokes that begin: *Doctor, doctor, …*
– Jokes that begin: *Waiter, waiter, …*
– Jokes asking questions about elephants, for example: *How do you know when an elephant has been in the fridge?* (Answer on page 172)
– Jokes that ask: *Why is X like Y?*
– Jokes that ask: *What is* (followed by a description), e.g. *What is black and white but read all over?* (Answer on page 172)

Do jokes with similar formats exist in your language?

2 ☐ Listen to the tape. Some people who work at a bank are discussing a magazine which they are producing for their branch of the bank. They want to include some jokes and are looking at some joke books and trying to get some ideas together.

These are the key words from each of the jokes they suggest. Look at the list and answer the questions below.

pilots in an old plane	cat and match
pancakes	elephant in bed
elephant under bed	elephant in fridge
elephant on fence	bear with no ears
Rupert the Bear	pig and ink
thief taking a bath	waterproof label
deer with no eyes	deer with no eyes and no legs
pawnbroker and gunman	old man's leg
beetle in gravy	kicks from job
fly in soup	

a Which of the jokes can you remember?

b Which did you find funny?

c Which did you not understand? Listen again. Can someone else in the class explain it to you if it is still not clear?

Vocabulary: Puns

1 English is very rich in homophones (words which sound the same but differ in meaning and sometimes spelling). This means that the language has a lot of scope for jokes based on punning or playing with words. Which of the jokes on the tape are based on a pun or a play on words?

2 There is a pun at the heart of each of the jokes below. Explain the pun in each case.

a Having asked for shelter for the night at a monastery the traveller was surprised and delighted at being given a magnificent supper of succulent fish and chips. 'That was absolutely magnificent,' he enthused to the monk who had been serving him. 'Not only was that piece of fish superb and beautifully cooked, but the chips … Never have I tasted better chips. Well done, Brother.' 'It would be better were you to thank Brother Ambrose for those,' came the reply. 'I'm the fish friar, he's the chip monk.'

b Clarence the crab called to see his friend Squizzy the squid.
'Gee, Squizzy. You look terrible. Are you okay?'
'No. I'm not okay; I feel awful,' answered Squizzy.
'We must do something,' said Clarence. 'For a start, it won't do you any good just lying there on the sea bed. We'll go for a walk. Were you to have a change of scenery and fresh water, that would put new life into you.'
They set off. Before long up swam a big crayfish.
'Here comes my bookie, Fred. Come and I'll introduce you,' said Clarence.
When they got closer, Clarence hailed the crayfish.
'Good morning, Fred. How are you? How's business?'
They talked for a while, then Clarence said:
'By the way, Fred. Here's the sick squid I owe you.'

c Doctor Bell fell down the well
And broke his collarbone;
A doctor should attend the sick
And leave the well alone.

d Did you hear the one about the farmer's boy who hated the country? Off went the boy to the big city and got a job as a shoe-shine boy. So the father made hay while the son shone.

3 Here are some more examples of jokes using the formats identified in Listening Exercise 1. Match the first line on the left with the second line on the right.

What's the difference between a tramp and a duvet?	Miss most of the film.
Doctor, doctor, I think I'm shrinking.	A hamburglar.
What would you do if an elephant sat in front of you at the cinema?	Try this bacon.
What are white, furry and taste of peppermints?	One's hard up, the other's soft down.
What do you call a nine-foot budgie?	Here you are. Use a magnifying glass.
Waiter, waiter, I can't see my steak.	Swedes.
What do you call a meat thief?	Polo bears.
Doctor, doctor, I need something for my liver.	Because it's in the middle of day.
How do elephants communicate?	You'll just have to be a little patient.
What's the difference between an elephant and a biscuit?	You can't dunk an elephant in your tea.
Why is the letter A like noon?	Sir.
What do vegetarian cannibals eat?	By elephone.

4 Here are some more English words which are homophones written in the IPA. Write them out in the two or more different ways in which each can be written.

eə   beə   greɪt   məʊn   preɪ
raɪt   siːm   saɪd   təʊd   weɪl

5 Now write sentences using each of the homophones in each set.

Example: *The heir to the throne took a breath of fresh air.*

6 Extended homophones are at the heart of a kind of joke that occasionally comes into fashion – pretend book titles by authors with appropriate names. Match the title with the author and explain the pun in each case.

Example
Unforeseen Problems by Major Setback
This is a pun on the word 'Major', which can either be a military title or can mean 'significant'.

Top ten books of the week
1	*The Bank Raid* by	Willie Winn
2	*The Millionaire* by	Mona Lott
3	*How to Cross the Road* by	M. T. Head
4	*The Jockey* by	Nora Bone
5	*So Tired* by	Dinah Mite
6	*Keeping Cheerful* by	Belle Ringer
7	*In the Lion's Den* by	J. Walker
8	*The Idiot* by	I. C. Waters
9	*Aching Arms* by	Carrie Mee
10	*The Arctic* by	Ivor Fortune

7 With a partner suggest book titles for the following authors. Which pair thinks of the best title for each of the authors?

a I. Sleep   **c** T. Thyme   **e** I. Steele
b R. U. Reddy   **d** Ivan Orange   **f** Rhoda Winner

Grammar: Word order

The basic word order of a sentence in English is, of course:
Subject – verb – object – adverbials of manner – place – time.
as in the sentence:
The traveller ate a delicious dinner with great relish at the monastery last night.
However, there are plenty of variations on this basic pattern.

1 Look at these sentences. In what ways does their word order vary from the standard pattern and when are these new word order patterns acceptable?

a 'No, I'm not OK; I feel awful,' answered Squizzy.
b Before long, up swam a big crayfish.
c Never have I tasted better chips.
d Were you to have a change of scenery and fresh water, that would put new life into you.

2 Find another example of each of these four varieties of word order pattern in Vocabulary Exercise 2, stories a–d.

3 Arrange the words in each set to form at least two different sentence patterns.

a the the off children park went to
b the no we rain gone down sooner came had than outside
c walked as as Sarah brass in bold
d when went came the the new old in out filing secretary system
e the go what you we need shop back buy really to to

What effect do the different word order patterns have on the sentences?

4 In Unit 15 we looked at the practice in spoken English of having a very long introductory noun phrase introducing the subject of a sentence. A frequent variation of this is to have a noun phrase describing the subject and then a pronoun as the subject of the sentence. Here are two examples:

That little girl next door, she complained to her mum, 'Simon's broken my doll!' Her mum asks, 'How did he do that?' and she says, 'I hit him on the head with it.'

You know that young history teacher, the one we saw in the supermarket last night? She asked Mario today what an archaeologist is and Mario said, 'Someone whose career is in ruins.'

An archaeologist is someone whose career is in ruins

5 Invent long introductory phrases for the following. Make them as original and as complex as you can.

a .... she asked Sally why she could never answer any of her questions in the lessons and she said, 'If I could, what would be the point of coming here?'

b .... he asked his son what he'd learnt in school today and the kid said, 'I learnt that those sums you did for me last night were all wrong.'

c .... she told the waiter that she'd like some tea without milk. The waiter said they hadn't got any milk, how about some tea without cream.

d .... they told us the one about the difference between a sick horse and a dead bee. One is a seedy beast and the other is a bee deceased.

6 Probably the commonest word order error in English is with the placing of adverbs and adverbial phrases. Put the phrase in brackets into the most appropriate position in the sentence.

a I like water-skiing. (very much)
b His new car is breaking down. (always)
c Could you tell me the way to the theatre? (possibly)
d We all enjoyed the jokes. (thoroughly)
e Jenny goes abroad for her work. (hardly ever)
f Could you please read the last paragraph? (aloud)
g We liked staying miles from anywhere for a week. (quite)
h We were asked to leave the room. (hurriedly)
i They wanted us to leave three books on the table. (only)
j Alec wants to finish that job. (badly)
k You will learn to appreciate his qualities one day. (perhaps)
l The Bakers are unable to come to our party. (unfortunately)

Speaking: Telling jokes

1 Discuss these questions with a partner and then compare your answers with those of other students in the class.

a Do you know anyone who is particularly good at telling jokes?
b What makes some people better at telling jokes than others are?

2 🔊 Listen to the same joke told by different people and answer the questions.

a Which person tells the joke more effectively?
b Why is this telling more effective?

3 On the tape at the beginning of the unit, did you notice how sometimes when the first part of the joke is a question, one of the listeners repeated the question?

For example:
What's the difference between a cat and a match?
I don't know. What's the difference between a cat and a match?

A comedy team often needs a 'straight man'. This person must try to be dead-pan as the joke is being told. What do you think the terms *straight man* and *dead-pan* mean?

Work with a partner. Try to recall some of the question and answer jokes from earlier in this unit – or, better still, others you know from elsewhere. Tell them to each other, with the listener acting as straight man and repeating the question as in the example above.

4 Work on telling a joke effectively in English yourself. Follow these instructions.

1 Choose a joke – preferably one you have heard or read outside the classroom. If you can't think of one, then choose one from earlier on in this unit.
2 Think about how to tell your joke. Which words would you need to stress? Where would you need to pause?
3 Record your joke.
4 Listen to the recordings of all the jokes and give each joke a grade out of five for content and out of five for presentation.

The main aspects of language worked on in this unit are:
- reading academic texts
- pronunciation of numbers
- complex sentences in academic texts
- formal linking words and expressions
- putting things in your own words

Warm-up: What changes the world?

1 Some objects and inventions have clearly exerted a very important influence on the development of society. Answer the questions below in groups and then compare your answers with those of other students.

a In what ways have the following affected society, in your opinion?
– the aeroplane   – antibiotics   – salt

b Name three other things which have changed society in some way. What changes have they made?

2 Look at the picture. It is called *The Potato Eaters* and is by Van Gogh. Answer these questions about it.

a What do you think are the characteristics of the people in the painting which the artist wanted to portray?

b What are the main characteristics of the potato as a food?

Reading: The social influence of the potato

1 You are going to read a rather unusual text from a very long history textbook devoted entirely to the potato and its influence on society. First think about these questions.

a The potato was not introduced into England until the sixteenth century, around the time of William Shakespeare. Can you suggest any ways in which its introduction might have changed society?

b In general, do you think it would have had a predominantly positive or a predominantly negative influence on society? Why?

2 Now read the first part of the text once and answer the
questions below.

a What are the two main characteristics of the potato which the
writer singles out?
b Are these characteristics only of benefit to the poorer members
of society?
c What is the potato's influence on society which the writer
describes in this text?
d Why is the potato able to have such an influence?
e In what kinds of society does the potato not have the sort of
influence described?

If for any reason, good or bad, conscious or otherwise, it is in the interests of one
economically stronger group to coerce another, then in the absence of political, legal or
moral restraint, that task is enormously facilitated when the weaker group can either be
persuaded or forced to adopt some simple, cheaply produced food as the mainstay of its
subsistence. Experience shows that this course inevitably results in a lower standard of
living. The lower that standard, the easier is the task of exploitation and the nearer will be
the status of the weaker class to serfdom. The potato, being the cheapest and one of the most
efficient single foods man has as yet cultivated in the temperate zones, lends itself readily to
the task of solving labour problems, along certain well-defined lines, in a society which, for
any reason, is already stratified into social classes. Whenever, therefore, the potato wins an
important, and still more, a dominant position in the diet of the people, it behoves us to ask
ourselves the question: what part is it playing in the economic scheme, and what is the risk
society is taking in encouraging or suffering a continuance of the same?

The potato can, and generally does, play a twofold part: that of a nutritious food, and
that of a weapon ready forged for the exploitation of a weaker group in a mixed society.

3 Now read the second part of the text and take notes on what
you read.

It is obvious that if a foodstuff is to be used as an instrument of exploitation, the more
valuable and acceptable it is as a food, the more effective will it be. Hence the richer nature's
gift, be it potatoes, rice or maize, the more extreme the contrast between its dual activities,
feeding and exploiting.

In a society wedded to the doctrine of *laissez-faire*, the problems of coercing the
politically weaker labourer in the interests of the politically protected employer were
determined in the main by the labourer's cost of subsistence; a potato diet was capable of
reducing that cost to the lowest level. Hence, it was in the employers' interests to urge the
use of the potato on the worker, which he did directly the cost of subsistence called for an
increased wage. It may be that it is seldom a cheap food that is designedly forced on
European workers, with a view of lowering their wages, but the potato has certainly been
used, and that of set purpose, with the view of preventing them from rising.

There are other factors – competition for labour, freedom or otherwise of
communication, doctrines whether religious, racial or national, tending to the greater or
lesser stratification of society – each of which can influence the application of the
instrument of exploitation, of which the potato affords an extreme example.

In the rare case of a society such as that of Tristan da Cunha, where there are no
economic motives for the exploitation of one group or class over another, or alternatively,
where the society has always been classless, the almost exclusive use of the potato has had
no evil social effect. Similarly, where, as in the Channel Islands, potatoes are raised in great
quantities for export, in the economic interest of the great majority of the community,
there need be no adverse social repercussion.

4 Now read the next part of the text and complete the table below.

	Late 18th century	Early 19th century (after French war)
General economic situation in Scottish Lowlands and North of England		
Effects of potato on that situation		

A different type of situation to either of the above developed during the latter part of the 18th and the earlier part of the 19th centuries in the Lowlands of Scotland and the northern counties of England. In both these regions the potato had been long established as an article of the people's daily food and had reduced their cost of living. But here its influence as an instrument of exploitation was, at an early stage, largely neutralised owing to the competition of the mines and the ironworks for labour. Nevertheless, the potato, by its cheapness as well as its nutritious qualities did, unknown either to worker or employer, effectively prevent any pronounced rise of wage in either the Lowlands or the north of England at the time of the corn shortage at the end of the 18th century. The danger of a potato economy was there, but it only showed itself when local industry as a whole was temporarily paralysed by the collapse of foreign markets in the early 1800s after the French wars.

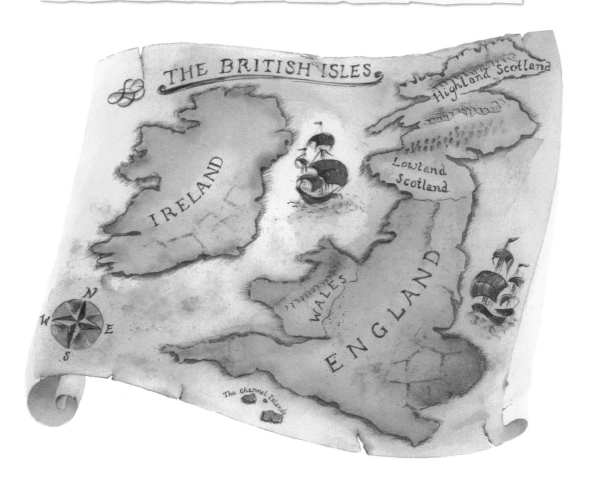

5 Now read the final part of the text and answer the questions your teacher asks you.

> When absence of competition is associated with a high degree of isolation, as it was in the Highlands of Scotland, then the potato can be, and in fact did become, the perfect instrument of exploitation, an exploitation so ruthless that it ended in the emigration of the greater part of the local working population. When later the Highlands were developed in the interests of grouse-shooting and deer-stalking, exploitation of labour as such ceased; but the low standard which had been acquired in the early 19th century remained, and can be seen today amongst the remnant which has not found employment as gillies or the like.
>
> In Ireland where, at the advent of the potato in about 1590, society was already hopelessly disintegrated, it met with no resistance and became in the shortest possible time the food of the people. In an environment poisoned by religious jealousies, undermined by political dissension, where industry was hamstrung at the dictate of an alien power, all the factors were to hand which made it inevitable that the use of the potato, cheapest of foods, would reduce the standard of living to the lowest level ever attained in Europe. After proving itself the most perfect instrument for the maintenance of poverty and degradation amongst the native masses, the potato ended in wrecking both exploited and exploiter.
>
> Thus man's wisdom, or his lack of it, alone decides whether even the richest of nature's gifts shall serve as a blessing or a curse.

6 Now read the text again and decide whether these statements are true or false. If the statements are false, explain why.

a Keeping workers' standard of living low enables employers to exploit employees.

b The characteristics of the potato as a food are such that eating it as a staple dulls the senses of its consumers, making them more easily exploitable.

c The potato is the only food which has had the effect the writer is describing on society.

d A society based on the concept of *laissez-faire* is less likely to lead to the potato being a tool of exploitation.

e Encouraging workers to eat potatoes was deliberately used as a method of social control in Europe.

f The potato has not had a harmful influence in Tristan da Cunha and the Channel Islands because they are both examples of classless societies, according to the writer.

g In the 1790s and the 1800s there was a range of employment opportunities throughout Scotland.

h In Ireland, those who exploited the potato were themselves ultimately destroyed by it too.

7 Follow the instructions to help you learn some of the new vocabulary in the text.

1 Choose ten new words or expressions from the text that you would like to have in your active vocabulary.
2 Write them in your vocabulary notebook in any appropriate way.
3 Write them in sentences of your own which illustrate their meaning.

Speaking: Pronunciation of numbers

Numbers are common in academic texts. You will frequently find statistical information, measurements, equations and other uses of numbers in scholarly books and articles. It can be surprisingly difficult even at an advanced level to process numbers that you hear and to say them accurately yourself. Practise with the following exercises.

1 Read these numbers aloud.

a 1590 AD
b 1902 AD
c the 1800s
d the 1990s
e 21 July
f 18th
g 12th
h £464
i 2,689 people
j 127 children
k $8,135
l $1/5$
m $2/3$
n $7/8$
o 0.726
p 12.07
q 519/18
r 123^2
s 123^7

📼 Now listen to the tape and check.

2 Now read these aloud. Then write them out in words.

a 2 + 3 = 5
b 789 + 693 = 1,482
c 6 − 2 = 4
d 3,361 − 554 = 2,807
e 3 × 9 = 27
f 19 × 25 = 475
g 475 ÷ 25 = 19
h Henry VIII had 6 wives.
i My phone number is 01223 240754.
j The room is 3m × 2.5m.
k The temperature today will rise to 37.7 ° C.
l Could you give me a £5 note?
m We're planning a 10km walk.
n The result of the football match was Rangers 0 Celtic 3.
o And in the tennis, the score is 15–0 to Maria.
p Sometimes the temperature in winter falls to 40° below 0.
q His grandfather was born in 1900 and died in 1992.
r His date of birth is August 6 1978.
s She earns $50,000 p.a.
t My e-mail address is 31245@cityscape.co.uk.

📼 Check what you have written with the tape.

3 📼 Listen to the sentences on the tape and write them down.

Grammar: Complex sentences

Academic texts in any discipline are often concerned with making comparisons between what happens in different circumstances and forming general observations. A useful construction for doing this is exemplified three times in the text on potatoes. Here are two of those examples.

The lower that standard (of living), the easier is the task of exploitation and the nearer will the status of the weaker class approximate to serfdom.

It is obvious that if a foodstuff is to be used as an instrument of exploitation, the more valuable and acceptable it is as a food, the more effective it will be.

Note that the comparatives used in sentences like these can be either adjectives or adverbs.

The older you get, the wiser you become.
The faster you do your work, the sooner we can go out.

Notice also that sentences using this construction can be re-worded so that it means *almost* the same using an *if* or a *when* sentence, e.g.
When employees' standard of living is low, then it is easier for bosses to exploit them and their position becomes closer to that of serfdom.

If a foodstuff is valuable and acceptable as a food to the population, then it is more effective as a tool of exploitation.

When you get older, you get wiser.

If you do your work fast, then we will be able to go out sooner than if you do it slowly.

Note that *when* conveys a more definite, universally true idea than *if*, which is used when the situation is less generally true. Sometimes the two are interchangeable.

1 Find the third example of the construction of this type in the text. (Clue: look in the second section of the text.)

2 Here are examples of halves of sentences using this construction. Complete them in any way that seems appropriate.

a The harder a student works, …
b The longer you stay at school, …
c …, the more popular his or her lectures will be.
d The more I play tennis with John, …
e …, the less likely that they will win the next general election.
f The higher the rate of unemployment, …
g …, the more she enjoys travelling.
h The more automated our society becomes, …

3 Go through the sentences you completed in the previous exercise. Reword them as *when* or *if* constructions.

4 Write three sentences of the type you practised in Exercise 2, relating to your own particular study discipline or area of current interest.

5 Another construction which is frequently used in academic writing is the use of *which* as a relative pronoun summing up what has been stated in the previous part of the sentence. For example:

Hence, it was in the employers' interest to urge the use of the potato on the worker, which he did directly the cost of subsistence called for an increased wage.

In speech or less formal writing *and this* is often used to replace *which*.

It was in the employers' interest to urge the use of the potato on the worker and this he did directly the cost of subsistence called for an increased wage.

Note that in academic texts *which* clauses used to sum up or comment on what has just been said will often continue in ways like this:
… which means that …
… which implies that …
… which suggested that …
… which led to …
… which was understandable since …
… which was a problem because …

Complete the following sentences in any appropriate way using *which* clauses which relate back to the main clause in its entirety as in the example. In the first two instances, one suggestion is already included. Write down an alternative ending.

a We parted knowing that we were unlikely ever to meet again, *which made me in particular very sad.* / …
b After the exams were over he felt very relieved, *which was understandable as he had been expecting to find the papers much more difficult.* / …
c The scientific team conducted a range of experiments into the behaviour of chimpanzees, …
d During the flight we ran into a lot of turbulence, …

e Girls are more likely to succeed at school than boys although more boys gain first-class university degrees, …
f On Tuesday my parents are setting off for Paris and, after a few days there, they will be heading for Venice, …

6 With a partner write three examples of sentences using *which* in the way practised above about your experiences this week. For example:

We've played a lot of squash together this week, which has been enjoyable but exhausting.

Compare your sentences with those written by other students.

7 In Unit 15 we looked at ellipsis in spoken English. Here are three examples of ellipsis from the text. Look at them and explain:

a The elliptical phrases in the first example have been underlined. What are the elliptical phrases in the other two examples?
b Reword each example without any ellipsis.
c Why do you think writers use ellipsis in academic and other texts?

The potato can, and generally <u>does</u>, play a twofold part: <u>that of</u> a nutritious food and <u>that of</u> a weapon <u>ready forged</u> for the exploitation of a weaker group in a mixed society.

In a society wedded to the doctrine of laissez-faire, *the problem of coercing the politically weaker labourer in the interests of the politically protected employer was simple, given a suitable instrument with which to bring it about.*

In an environment poisoned by religious jealousies, undermined by political dissension, where industry was hamstrung at the dictate of an alien power, all the factors were to hand which made it inevitable that the use of the potato, cheapest of foods, would reduce the standard of living to the lowest level ever attained in Europe.

8 These sentences are rather clumsy because they do not make any use of ellipsis. Rewrite them using ellipsis where possible.

a He intended to write a history of the religions of the world but he had not even started writing his history of the religions of the world before he fell ill and he died two months later.

b Potatoes are a very flexible food in that you can eat roast potatoes, mashed potatoes, potatoes in their jackets and indeed you can enjoy potatoes which have been cooked in a wide range of other ways.

c Even if the government had been able to abolish unemployment, it probably would not have abolished unemployment.

d A tunnel which would run under the Channel and which would link Britain and France had been discussed for over a century before it was finally built.

e The zoologist noticed that stores of nuts had not been laid up for the winter as they should have been laid up for the winter.

f They would have liked to buy a more powerful computer to process their data but they could not afford to buy a more powerful machine.

g They have three large cupboards which are crammed with antique china and antique glass.

h My role is to collect the information; my role is not to interpret the information which has been collected.

9 Choose a special page in your file or notebook and collect some examples of ellipsis.

1 Find two more examples of ellipsis in the text and write them out in an expanded way.

2 If you are reading any other texts at the moment, try to find some examples of ellipsis there too.

Vocabulary: Formal linking words and expressions

The writer of this text uses a number of rather formal connecting words and expressions.

1 Look at the examples. Replace the underlined words or expressions by less formal equivalents. This may involve making other changes to the sentences as well.

a <u>Hence</u>, the richer nature's gift, the more extreme the contrast between its dual activities, feeding and exploiting.

b … nature's gift, <u>be</u> it potatoes, rice or maize, …

c Wages, <u>in the absence of</u> any protective mechanism, were determined <u>in the main</u> by the labourer's cost of subsistence.

d In the rare case of a society such as Tristan da Cunha, where there are no economic motives for the exploitation of one class over another, or <u>alternatively</u>, where the society has always been classless, the almost exclusive use of the potato has had no evil social effect. <u>Similarly</u> where, as in the Channel Islands, potatoes are raised in great quantities for export, in the economic interest of the great majority of the community, there need be no adverse social repercussion.

e But here its influence as an agent of exploitation was, at an early stage, largely neutralised <u>owing to</u> the competition of the mines and the ironworks for labour. <u>Nevertheless</u> the potato, by its cheapness, as well as its nutritious qualities, did … effectively prevent any pronounced rise of wage in either the Lowlands of Scotland or the north of England …

f <u>Thus</u> man's wisdom, or his lack of it, alone decides whether even the richest of nature's gifts shall serve as a blessing or a curse.

2 Write sentences relating to a discipline that you are studying or have studied. Try to use each of the underlined words or expressions from Exercise 1.

Speaking: Two academic games

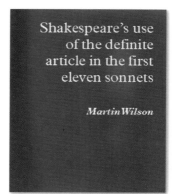

Shakespeare's use of the definite article in the first eleven sonnets

Martin Wilson

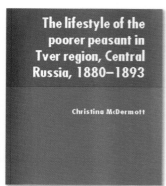

The lifestyle of the poorer peasant in Tver region, Central Russia, 1880–1893

Christina McDermott

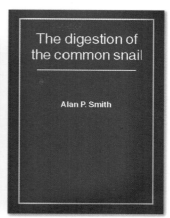

The digestion of the common snail

Alan P. Smith

1 *The History and Social Influence of the Potato* is perhaps an unlikely title for a book with over six hundred pages. Yet academics often spend years studying subjects which seem very specialised and possibly of little interest to ordinary people.

Follow these instructions.

1 Work with a partner and write down three titles for doctoral theses which seem to you to be the epitome of academic dryness.
2 Choose one of the titles you thought up and compare it with those of other pairs.
3 Each choose one of your titles and present it to the class. Imagine that you are trying to persuade a research council to give you a grant to carry out this particular piece of research. Discuss some potential arguments for each of your topics with your partner.
4 Argue your case as plausibly as you can.

2 Academics also enjoy knowing facts which may to the rest of us seem to be of little use. For example:

– The 5th most common surname in Britain is Taylor.
– There are 3,901 lines in Shakespeare's play *Hamlet* of which 1,422 are spoken by Hamlet himself.
– British men spend an average of 1 hour 29 minutes a day eating, whereas women spend only 1 hour 12 minutes.

Follow these instructions.

1 Write down five other 'Useless but true facts' using an encyclopaedia or any other book or magazine to help you, if you wish.
2 Work in a group of three students. Read out your facts to each other. Decide which fact to put forward as your entry in the 'finals'.
3 Read out the fact selected by your group.

Study skills: Putting it in your own words

When you are working with academic texts, you are often asked to express something in your own words. This means that you have to convey the same ideas using different vocabulary items as far as is possible but without changing the meaning.

Clearly, you first have to make sure that you are absolutely clear about what the original text means; only then can you begin to try to re-word the writer's ideas.

The other prerequisite for doing this task well is to have a good vocabulary. Make a point not only of learning words which relate specifically to your own discipline but also make sure that you learn words and expressions which can be useful in a range of academic texts.

If you need to practise this skill, try the following two exercises.

1 Write the first paragraph of the text at the beginning of the unit in your own words.

2 Choose a short text in English from your own discipline and put it into your own words. Discuss your 'translation' with your teacher.

19 | Business class
Business advice

The main aspects of language worked on in this unit are:	• understanding business English • speaking at meetings • emphasis through grammar • the vocabulary of meetings • guessing meaning from context

Warm-up: Business English

Look at the activities in the box and answer the questions below.

> giving a presentation
> making small talk at a work-related function
> negotiating a sale
> participating in a meeting
> reading business articles
> showing a colleague from abroad around your workplace
> talking on the telephone
> writing a report
> writing business letters

a Which of the activities in the box above have you already had some experience of in your own language?

b For which of the activities in the box have you already had some experience of using English?

c For which of them do you think you may well need to use English in the future?

d Which have you found – or do you think you would find – easiest and which most difficult? Why?

e Have you come across any differences in the way English speakers approach these activities than people from your own country?

f Do you think cultural differences can be important when doing business?

Listening: Negotiating

1 You are going to listen to part of a self-study tape for business people. The tape aims to teach them how to negotiate a sale successfully. Before you listen, discuss these questions with a partner.

a What sorts of advice do you think the tape might offer on successful negotiation?

b What techniques do you think the producers of the tape might use to make the tape more interesting and effective as a self-study method?

2 🖭 Now listen to the tape and answer these questions.

a To what extent were your predictions in Exercise 1 correct?

b What comments would you make about the 'lesson' given on the tape? Did you think the advice it gave was useful?

3 Here is a dialogue between two people negotiating a sale. Tick the parts of the dialogue that are in accordance with the advice given on the tape and mark with a cross those parts of the dialogue which go against the advice on the tape. Correct the latter sections in accordance with the advice given and, if possible, with your own knowledge of sales negotiation.

MR BROWN: Good morning. Nice to meet you again. Did you have a good journey?

MS BLACK: Yes, thanks. Now, let's get straight down to business. I'm sure your time is as valuable as mine is. I understand you want to increase your order for our ballpoint pens but that you feel you should get a discount for bulk ordering. I must start by telling you that I really can't offer you much of a discount. We've been selling you these pens at very low profit margins as it is.

MR BROWN: Then how come McDonald's can offer us a considerably lower price on a similar product?

MS BLACK: Well, their products are pretty shoddy, aren't they? Tell me what exactly you have in mind as a discount.

MR BROWN: We thought ten per cent would be reasonable.

MS BLACK: You must be kidding. I couldn't possibly consider anything like that. Three per cent is really all I can offer you. Otherwise we'd be selling at a loss.

MR BROWN: In that case, I think we'll go to McDonald's.

MS BLACK: I'm sure you'll regret it. Well, I'll be off then. I'll get in touch with you in six months' time in case you want to come back to us.

4 Work with a partner and follow these instructions.

1 You are going to role play a sales negotiation. Decide what you are selling, who is the sales person and who the purchaser.

2 Act out a sales negotiation situation following the advice given on the tape.

3 Report back to your class on how your role play went and on any problems you encountered.

Grammar: Emphasis

1 Here are 16 different examples of ways of emphasising, all of which have come from a business context. Follow these instructions.

1 Explain what was done in each case to make the statement more emphatic.
2 Reword each sentence so that emphasis is not used.

a I do appreciate your concerns.
b Whatever has happened to the price of their shares?
c Nobody at all would choose to work for that company if they had any other options.
d He wouldn't get anything whatsoever done if his secretary didn't arrange it all for him.
e What she did was decide where she wanted to be in the company in two years' time and then she set about getting there as quickly as she could.
f In no other company have I experienced such a strong feeling of corporate identity.
g I myself don't see the point of the chairman's new proposal.
h Last week's shareholders' meeting was excruciatingly boring.
i Although she was an absolute novice when she arrived two months ago, she is now one of our star workers.
j What Jones and Co. claimed at the meeting was an outright lie.
k Although he receives an excellent salary he has to work dreadfully hard to get it.
l James is *the* man to talk to about your proposal.
m The meeting finished just as the clock struck seven.
n It was Katie who had the initial idea for the project.
o What we should go on to do next is not quite certain.
p We had little chance of success, I thought.

2 Did you notice in examples i and j above how the adjectives *absolute* and *outright* were used to emphasise a point?

Here is a list of adjectives which can be used in this emphatic way.

absolute	complete	entire	outright	
perfect	positive	pure	real	total
true	utter			

Look in a good dictionary to see which nouns each of these words collocate with when they have a purely emphatic function and write down each word with two or more collocations, e.g. *a perfect stranger*, *a perfect idiot*.

3 Choose one of the following situations.

a a sales negotiation
b a job interview
c showing a colleague from the USA around your workplace

Write down sentences of your own about the situation you chose using three of these other techniques which were exemplified in Exercise 1.

a Using an auxiliary verb simply for emphasis, e.g. in a.
b Using a cleft sentence, e.g. e and n.
c Using inversion after a negative or restricting adverbial, e.g. f.
d Using an emphasising adverb, e.g. h and k.
e Fronting, i.e. putting what would normally come second first, e.g. o and p.
f Using *just* before *as*, e.g. m.
g Using one of the reflexive pronouns for emphatic effect, e.g. g.
h Using *at all* to emphasise a negative, e.g. c.
i Using *whatsoever* to emphasise a negative, e.g. d.

4 Compare your sentences with those written by other students. Write down any of the other students' sentences which you feel are particularly good examples.

Vocabulary: The language of business meetings

Follow the instructions in order to learn more about the language of business meetings.

1 Look at the list of 30 useful phrases for business meetings below.
2 With a partner, organise the phrases into groups in any way that seems logical to you. You might sequence the phrases from a time point of view, for example, considering at what point during a meeting they are likely to be used.
3 Compare the way you grouped the phrases with the groupings identified by other pairs.
4 Can you add any phrases to any of the groups identified?

1 Could we have a show of hands on this one?
2 Do we have a quorum?
3 Does anyone wish to raise anything in connection with the minutes?
4 I am speaking on behalf of …
5 I don't think that that is relevant to the discussion in hand.
6 I don't think we can take a decision on this until we have some further information.
7 I have three main points to make.
8 I see heads nodding in agreement.
9 I should like to propose a vote of thanks to …
10 I should like to take up on John's point that …
11 I think I speak for all of us when I say that …
12 Is there a consensus?
13 Is there any other business?
14 It is essential that we should come to some agreement today.
15 Let's put it on hold.
16 Mr Brown has been waiting to speak for some time.
17 One at a time, please.
18 Please let me finish.
19 Shall we agree to differ on that one?
20 Shall we shelve that for the time being?
21 The feeling of the meeting seems to be that …
22 The minutes of the last meeting have been circulated in advance.
23 There are a number of factors which we need to consider.
24 This is off the record.
25 We have a number of items on the agenda today which can be dealt with fairly rapidly.
26 We have apologies from …
27 We will not quote you verbatim.
28 We'll adjourn the meeting until …
29 With all due respect …
30 Would you address all remarks to the chair, please.

Reading: Advice for business people

1 Here are 10 more pieces of advice for business people taken from a book with 371 such pieces of advice for people wanting to make the most of their lives in business. Each piece of advice has been divided into two parts. Follow these instructions.

1 Find the continuation in the right-hand column for each of the pieces of advice begun in the left-hand column.
2 Explain in your own words each of the pieces of advice you identified.

Always tell the truth to employers and your boss;
Beware of those who ask for feedback;
Don't roll your eyes
Never get caught
Never go into partnership
When the outcome of a meeting is another meeting,
Every once in a while discuss the size of elves and leprechauns,
Always keep the ball
The purpose of the staff is
Go to the company picnic

and whether or not you believe in them, with your staff.
with a game on your computer screen.
it's been a lousy meeting.
with a friend.
in their court.
but don't stay long.
to make management jobs easier.
it's easier to remember what you said.
they are really asking for approval.
in meetings.

2 Here are the beginnings of six more such pieces of advice. How do you think they might have continued?

a If we had a penny for every company strategy we never actually implemented …
b The best way to derail a meeting is …
c Organisational change won't occur unless …
d If you take the last cup of coffee …
e Never use a cellular phone …
f Since we may be stuck wearing grey suits or other conservative clothes …

Speaking: Business meeting

You are now going to hold a business meeting in which you discuss the introduction of a new product to the company where you work. As you participate in this meeting, try to make use of some of the language of meetings which you have been working on in this unit.

Your company produces a range of novelties aimed at the business market. It has been very successful, for example, with a calendar which includes a weekly humorous comment on business. Other products which you make which sell well are telephone notepads, pens and car stickers with I ♥ Business on them.

You are now interested in developing some goods with some of the pieces of advice from *Reading* Exercises 1 and 2 on them.

A meeting has been called in which different groups will present their ideas to the Board. The manager of the company will chair the meeting, his or her secretary will take the minutes and the agenda for the meeting will be as follows:

Your teacher will give you instructions about what exactly you are going to do and about who is going to play which role in the meeting.

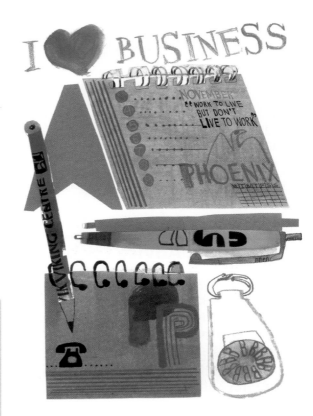

AGENDA
1   Apologies
2   Minutes of last meeting
3   Presentation of new product ideas from groups
4   Discussion of these ideas
5   Vote on which product to adopt
6   Vote on which slogan(s) to adopt
7   AOB

Study skills: Guessing meaning from context

If you have a business background, you may find it easier to work out the meaning of some of the unfamiliar words in a text on a business-related subject. The ability to guess meaning from context is a useful skill to practise and try to improve. The things which will help you work out the meaning of an unfamiliar word are:

a the meaning of the text which surrounds it;
b the way the word is formed;
c your own background knowledge of the subject.

1 You have probably never been taught the underlined words in these sentences. Use the context surrounding the word to help you work out what the word probably means. Then check the correct meaning with your teacher. How good were you at working out the meaning?

a The majority of animal species are <u>invertebrates</u> as 97% of all species do not have a spine.
b If you don't wear gloves outdoors in Scotland in winter, you may well get <u>chilblains</u>, which can be very itchy and uncomfortable.
c *Radar, level* and *madam I'm Adam* are examples of <u>palindromes</u>. One of the longest examples is *Doc, note, I dissent. A fast never prevents a fatness. I diet on cod.*
d <u>Catgut</u>, which was made from the intestines of sheep or horses rather than cats, has now largely been replaced by synthetic fibres in the strings of musical instruments.
e Don't forget to wipe your hands and mouth after eating such a <u>gooey</u> cream cake.

2 You have probably not seen the underlined words in these sentences before. Use the way the word has been formed to help you work out what it probably means. Then check the correct meaning with your teacher. How good were you at doing this?

a I am afraid you have been <u>misinformed</u> about the cost of our products.
b Britain was one of the countries involved in a <u>tripartite</u> project to improve business relations between East and West.
c Those expenses are all <u>tax-deductible</u>.
d I don't think this porcelain is <u>dishwasherproof</u>.
e The advertisement lists a string of <u>pseudo-facts</u> in an attempt to persuade people to buy the company's slimming products.

3 You have probably not previously come across the underlined words in these sentences. Use your own world knowledge to help you work out what the word probably means. Then check the correct meaning with your teacher. How good were you at doing this?

a Every day we spent in the Tropics, the heat was <u>blistering</u>.
b Postcards from Australia characteristically show either a kangaroo or a koala bear sitting on a <u>gum tree</u>.
c <u>Quills</u> were the main writing implement used in Europe from the 6th century AD to the advent of steel pens in the mid-nineteenth century.
d Sugar quickly <u>dissolves</u> in hot tea.
e A spider spins a <u>cobweb</u> in order to catch flies.

4 Practise all your skills of guessing words from context with this text. Follow these instructions.

1 As you read the text, underline all the words and expressions which you do not know.
2 Work out, using all the information you have from the context, its formation and your own background knowledge, what you think each word or expression means.
3 Check your 'guesses' in a dictionary. How close were you?
4 On looking at the text again, do you think that you could have got any closer to the meanings which you did not manage to work out satisfactorily?

Michael Lawrence, defenestrated

INCREASED turnover in shares is something that the London Stock Exchange loves to crow about. It must be far less proud about its turnover in chief executives. Barely two years ago, its previous boss fell on his sword after the exchange's attempts to create a paperless share-settlement system turned into a costly fiasco. Now the exchange has lost his replacement, Michael Lawrence, who was asked to leave by the board on January 4th. What does this mean for the exchange and for the City?

The main cause of the latest fiasco is a conflict between the modernisers, led by Mr Lawrence, who wanted to drag the exchange into the 21st century and several member firms that seem grimly determined to maintain the status quo. A quarrel over the future of London's quote-driven market, in which investors deal in shares via market-makers who make them bids and offers, brought matters to a head. Mr Lawrence and others felt that, in order to compete with other exchanges in an increasingly integrated European capital market, London needed to introduce order-driven trading, under which investors' buy and sell orders are automatically matched.

The appeal of order-driven trading is that it eliminates the need for a middleman. London's middlemen were unamused. Big market-making firms objected to Mr Lawrence's desire to introduce such a system alongside the existing one as part of the exchange's ongoing plans to update its trading platform.

Mr Lawrence's opponents blame him for failing to consult them sufficiently. His fans say that he did his best to convince Luddites that change was essential if the exchange was to cope with upstarts, such as Tradepoint, an order-driven trading service launched last year.

Mr Lawrence's departure is unlikely to solve the underlying question: what is the point of an exchange at all? Shares have not been physically traded in the exchange since London's Big Bang in 1986. It has also been stripped of its settlement role. Meanwhile its biggest members gripe that, while its role has diminished, the exchange's costs have not. The new man should bring his axe.

The main
aspects of
language
worked on in
this unit are:

- understanding humour
- gerunds and infinitives
- homographs
- writing an article for a class magazine

Warm-up: Humorous writing

1 Discuss these questions with the rest of the class.

a What books or other things have you read (in English or your own language) that have made you laugh – or at least smile to yourself? Brainstorm as many things as possible.

b What do these words have in common and what is different about each of them – *guffaw, titter, chuckle, fall about, grin*?

c Do any of these words describe how you react to any of the things you brainstormed in answer to the first question?

2 If possible work with a partner who has enjoyed the same humorous book or writer that you have and decide which of these characteristics the book or the writer have that make you laugh (or smile) as you read:

- humorous illustrations
- a farcical situation
- an amusing way of presenting everyday life
- an element of social or political satire
- an element of black humour
- something surreal about the story
- clever use of language (e.g. puns)
- use of irony
- use of exaggeration
- use of understatement
- something else – if so, what?

List the characteristics of humorous writing in order of importance for you personally. Compare the way you ordered the points with your partner's list. Then join another pair and compare the order which you each selected.

3 Much humour in English is based on a writer looking at everyday life from a gently humorous point of view. In this unit, you are going to read an example of this kind of humour. It is based on the relationship between a teenage girl and her mother. Before reading, discuss the following with a partner.

a Did or do you and your parents ever disagree about any of the following – clothes and appearance, friends, using the telephone, politics, work? If so, write down three things that your parents typically say when you are disagreeing about one of these topics. For example, *Those shoes will ruin your feet.*

b What sorts of things do young teenagers do with their money?

c What sorts of problems can money cause between teenagers and their parents? Try to think of the problem from the point of view both of the teenager and of the parent.

d Write a dialogue between a teenage girl and her mother. The teenager wants some money but her mother is reluctant to give it to her.

Reading: Treasure's pocket money

1 The article below is by Gina Davidson, the writer of a popular column in *The Guardian* newspaper. It is about the everyday life of a thirteen-year-old girl, Treasure, and her mother. The two live alone – but have regular visits to Grandma – and have a fairly stormy relationship.

Read the article and summarise its content in one sentence.

Treasure's pocket money

Treasure was born to spend. She therefore needs huge amounts of pocket money. It is her life blood, she can scarcely move without it. She spends it, lends it, donates it, loses it. She buys snacks, tickets, make-up, bargain offers and presents. She is a fountain of pocket money and I am the source of her wealth – the magic porridge pot. Treasure says the correct words and up comes more pocket money. Because without it she is a prisoner in the house, an unpleasant option for both of us.

'I must have some,' she begs. 'I need it. I had to pay all the taxi fares because no one else had any money. They're all going to pay me back.'

'Good. Then you'll have some money.'

'But I haven't got enough money to get to them.'

Treasure is at her wits' end. 'You don't understand how much I spend on fares.' She is addressing an ignoramus. 'Fares are very expensive.' Her needs are always pressing. This month has been particularly pressing because it was Peter's birthday and Chloe's birthday and she had to buy Easter eggs.

I am keen to know how much pocket money her friends get. Treasure doesn't know. Her friends don't know either. They become confused when asked. They don't even remember whether they have to earn it by doing the odd household task. This is a mysterious grey area.

Treasure is meant to do certain chores to earn her money. She doesn't refuse. She will do them, she promises, but she has other more urgent duties – dancing in her room, hugging the dog, phoning Rosie, going to sleep. In my weak way, I have not always enforced these rules. Naturally people have criticised. 'You're making a rod for your own back,' bellows Grandma. She compares her indolent grandchild to the girls who used to live next door. They were paragons in Grandma's eyes. They peeled potatoes, made beds, washed up, never answered back. Having given up on me, Grandma tries Treasure.

'There's only one thing I want you to do,' she begs Treasure in a tragic way. 'Just help your mother. That's all I ask you to do.'

This request always throws Treasure into a sullen fury. Grandma's wishes have never been realised. I continue to dole out pocket money regardless. But at least Treasure is a generous child. She spends the bulk of it on presents. I do rather well out of her pocket money. I even have a Teasmade. I have chocs, flowers, tapes and my birthdays are sumptuous affairs. Nevertheless I have cut the pocket money now and then when Treasure's behaviour has gone beyond the pale. But that ploy no longer works. Treasure has a new ally. The bank.

The wicked bank tempted Treasure with a cash card and tons of free gifts. It advertised on TV. All her saved-up birthday and Christmas present money can now be frittered with ease. The bank is eager for Treasure to join our nation of debtors and be one of them. It does not wish to encourage thrift. I am no match for such an opponent. I dream that one day when all Treasure's savings are gone and I am bankrupt, necessity will force me to be strict about pocket money.

Treasure must have read my mind. 'I don't want you to give me all my pocket money,' says she out of the blue. 'I want to save it. I want you to put it in this piggy bank in your room so I can't get it.' She stuffs a fiver into the pig. 'Can I have some advance pocket money? I need three pounds. I must have it.'

'But you've got that five.'

'I can't spend that,' says Treasure. 'I'm saving it.'

---

2 At certain points in this text, it is necessary to read between the lines in order fully to appreciate the gentle humour of the article. These questions check whether you have managed to read between the lines of the article.

a Why does Treasure's mother keep on giving her pocket money?

b Has this month been a particularly bad month for Treasure in terms of what she has had to spend?

c Why doesn't Treasure know how much her friends get for pocket money?

d Why do her friends become confused when Treasure's mother asks them whether they have to do household chores to earn their pocket money?

e Does Treasure have any intention of doing the household chores her mother expects of her?

f Why is Grandma critical of Treasure's mother?

g Has the bank behaved in the way Treasure's mother would have expected it to?

h Is Treasure's mother pleased that Treasure wants to start saving?

3 Think about the humour in the text. Mark three expressions or sentences or longer parts of the text which you find humorous in some way. Answer these questions.

a Which of the aspects of humour discussed in *Warm-up* Exercise 2 on page 143 can be found in this extract?
b Which of the laughing and smiling verbs which you discussed in *Warm-up* Exercise 1 on page 143 best fits the kind of humour in this text for you? Can you explain why the text is humorous?
c Do you think that the humorous way in which the situation is treated perhaps helps to make a potentially difficult situation easier for those involved?
d If so, do you think it is more helpful for either parents or teenagers? Why (not)?

4 Treasure and her mother live in North London. These articles are popular throughout Britain, however, because the situations and conversations are echoed in many homes all over the country. Answer these questions.

a Have you ever participated in or witnessed scenes similar to those described here in your own country? If not, do you think such scenes could occur in your country?
b If the text were going to be published in your country (in your language), would it need any particular footnotes to explain anything that would not be clear to anyone unfamiliar with English lifestyles? If so, where would notes be necessary and how could they be worded?

Vocabulary: Homographs

English has a great many words which have more than meaning for the same spelling. The word *bank*, for example, can refer to a place which keeps your money, the side of a river or to being confident that something will happen (*to bank on something*).

1 In the sentences below, the same word fits into a, b and c in each case. All the words you need can be found, with one or other of their meanings, in the *Treasure* text. Identify the word in each case.

1 a Our team is having a return .... with St John's First XV next week.
  b John is very bright but he's no .... for Stella.
  c Mother wants to make some curtains to .... the new wallpaper.
2 a If you would like to stand for the committee, I should be happy to .... you.
  b It can be easier to get into a tight parking place if you try to .... into it.
  c She ran out of the restaurant leaving her handbag hanging on the .... of her chair.
3 a My father always claimed that they serve better .... in many army kitchens than in a lot of expensive hotels.
  b The party is hoping to .... rather better in the next set of elections.
  c You can end up having to pay a hefty fine if you try to avoid paying your train ....

4 a It would be a good idea to .... those flowers and bring them indoors for the winter.
  b He would be quite attractive if it weren't for his .... belly.
  c I'll go and make a fresh .... of tea.
5 a That bull terrifies me when it .... although I'm told it has a very sweet nature.
  b Use the .... to get the fire going properly.
  c I think Grandma .... because she is a little deaf.
6 a In child custody cases the court usually .... in favour of the mother.
  b Before you move in with us, I think we should establish some ground ....
  c The change in the weather really .... out the possibility of a picnic this afternoon.
7 a How long are you going to go on attempting your driving test? You've had nine .... already.
  b Judge Grim often .... more complex cases in the appeal court.
  c His constant whingeing really .... my patience.

8 a If you seal the windows with sticky .... in the winter, you won't have so many draughts.

b I'm going to try to .... the concert tonight.

c Have you got a .... measure, please? I want to check the size of this rug before I buy it.

9 a The teacher marks all the children who are .... in the register.

b I've been invited to .... some flowers to the guest of honour.

c We can't do very much to help for the .... but perhaps later on we'll be able to do something.

10 a Although Jane looks quite ordinary, I find her a very .... person.

b Write down any three .... numbers.

c Jack is very useful when it comes to doing .... jobs around the house.

2 **You are now going to write your own sentences like those in Exercise 1 above. Follow these instructions.**

1 Your teacher will give you and a partner three words which have multiple meanings.

2 Using a dictionary to help you, write three sentences illustrating three different meanings for each of your words, but leave a gap in your sentences where the word should be.

3 Where possible use the word in different parts of speech, e.g. as a noun, verb and adjective where this is possible.

4 Make sure that you use the word in the same form each time, i.e. without adding any plural or verb ending.

5 Exchange sentences with other pairs of students and see how many of their words you can identify.

3 ▭ **Now answer these questions about homophones.**

a What is the difference between a homograph and a homophone?

b Can you think of any examples of homophones?

c Listen to the examples of homophones on the tape and write what you hear in at least two different ways.

Listening: More about Treasure

You are going to listen to another extract from an article about Treasure and her mother. This one is about Treasure's use of the telephone.

1 **Answer these questions before listening to the tape.**

a The article is written at the beginning of spring. How is spring traditionally said to affect people's behaviour?

b How do you think spring might affect the behaviour of the teenagers who live on Treasure's street?

c What do you think will be the problem with telephone use from the point of view of Treasure's mother?

d And what will be the problem from Treasure's point of view?

2 ▭ **Listen to the tape and answer these questions.**

a What could Treasure's mother see the neighbouring teenagers doing now that the light evenings of spring had arrived?

b Describe in detail the telephoning problem that Treasure and her mother have.

c At the end of the extract does Treasure's mother wish she had a son? Why (not)?

3 Look at the tapescript on page 173 and answer these questions.

a Why do you think the words *Go Out and Dump Them* are written with capital letters? Can you 'hear' the capital letters when the extract is read on tape? If so, how?

b If the text were to be published outside Britain it might need footnotes to explain the following:
– 18 plus videos
– upmarket
– peak time
– 38p a minute
How could those footnotes be worded?

4 Are the following extracts from the tape humorous, in your opinion? If so, why?

a An upmarket brand of youth can sometimes be seen lolling against the front garden walls employing a cordless telephone.

b She can have whole relationships without any physical contact.

c Once on it she loses track of time, even peak time.

d 'Everybody knows I've got a mother with red glasses who swears.'

e She hasn't quite understood my instructions, assuming not that she *may* use the phone between eight and nine but that she *must*.

f On the dot of eight she springs to it and phones like billy-oh.

5 Discuss with a partner.

a Are there any other ways apart from those discussed in the previous exercise in which humour is achieved in this extract?

b Can you think of any ways in which a similar kind of humour could be used to describe your situation either in class or at home at the moment?

6 Listening to (and reading) English can help you to have an instinctive feel for what is correct. Below there are some sentences from the *Treasure* extract you have just listened to. In each sentence there is at least one mistake – of grammar or vocabulary. Can you identify and correct the errors? Do not look at the tapescript (on page 173) until you have completed the exercise.

a It is spring and all along our street the teenagers are running muck.

b In the light evenings and through the open windows they can be seen and heard to shriek and to skulk.

c I've tried limiting her telephoning. Between eight and nine was being Treasure's phoning time.

d Nobody else's mother is so nasty and spoonful.

e She is deep ashamed for me.

f If I should use the phone even briefly during her time, Treasure is incensing.

Grammar: *-ing* forms and infinitives

1 Think about how and why *-ing* forms and infinitives are used in the texts you have been working on.

Go through both the listening and the reading texts and underline all the examples of

a *-ing* forms
b infinitives.

Explain why the *-ing* form or infinitive is used in each case.

2 These words can take either the *-ing* form or the infinitive:

> allow begin bother cease forget go on hate intend like mean need permit regret remember start stop try want

Divide these verbs into three groups:

a those that take either the infinitive or the *-ing* form depending on the stylistic preferences of the speaker.

b those that take either the infinitive or the *-ing* form depending on the context.

c those that take either the infinitive or the *-ing* form depending on the meaning of the verb in the particular context.

3 Write sentences which show how the verbs in groups b and c are used with 1 the infinitive and 2 the *-ing* form.

Writing: Articles for a class magazine

You are now coming to the end of this book and probably the end of a course. Preparing a class magazine can be an enjoyable way both to recall some of the activities you have enjoyed as a group and to work on your English at the same time.

If the articles in the magazine are written in a humorous vein, then the magazine may be a particularly enjoyable souvenir.

You are going to prepare a class magazine in which each student – or pair of students – writes an article. Follow these instructions.

1 Discuss what subjects would make interesting articles for the magazine. Tick any of the following subjects which would be suitable.
   ☐ Ideas on how to spend the weekend – without spending too much money, perhaps
   ☐ Outstanding memories of your course
   ☐ Amusing experiences of learning English
   ☐ Pen portraits of your classmates (or teachers?)
   ☐ Review of a book, film or sports event you have recently read or watched
   ☐ Advice for people considering different careers
   ☐ Discussion of a personal problem
   ☐ Comment on the English sense of humour
   ☐ Report of and comment on a recent news event
   ☐ Report of an interview
   ☐ Report of the findings of an opinion poll or questionnaire
   ☐ Crossword and/or other puzzles
   ☐ Cartoons or jokes
   ☐ Poems
   Add any other ideas appropriate for your class.
2 Choose a title for the magazine.
3 Decide who is going to write which article – and who is going to design the title page.
4 Plan your article. Look back at some of the aspects of humorous writing that we have discussed in this unit and think how some of them might be incorporated into your article.
5 Write the article. Aim particularly at having an interesting beginning and ending and at trying both to amuse and to hold your readers' interest throughout.

6 Show your article to another student – or pair of students – and ask them:
   a) to tell you about any mistakes they see
   b) to suggest ways of making the article more amusing or interesting.
7 Write or, if possible, type a final version of your article.
8 Make sure that all the members of the class read the magazine. You could divide it into sections, for ease of distribution, and pass it round the class or you could display it on the wall in the classroom.
If you have the facilities, make extra copies of the magazine so that several people can read it at the same time.

21 | A compelling read
Blurbs

The main aspects of language worked on in this unit are:	• reading blurbs • writing – presenting characters • prepositions • the language of publicity • suggested further reading

Warm-up: Reading tastes

1 What sorts of things do you enjoy reading in your own language?

Give each of the following a rating from 1 to 5 – where 5 = I enjoy reading this sort of thing very much and 1 = I get no pleasure at all from reading this sort of thing.

Type of publication	Rating	Example
newspapers	☐	*The Times, The International Herald Tribune*
magazines (specify which kind)	☐	*Time, New Scientist*
comic books	☐	Charles Schulz (*Peanuts*)
textbooks (specify what kind)	☐	depends on subject
science fiction	☐	Ray Bradbury, Arthur C Clarke
(auto)biography	☐	Antonia Fraser
poetry	☐	Oxford or Penguin anthologies
romantic fiction	☐	Catherine Cookson, Danielle Steel
classical novels	☐	R L Stevenson, Jane Austen
modern classics	☐	Margaret Drabble, Doris Lessing
humour	☐	Sue Townsend, Alan Coren
detective stories	☐	Agatha Christie, Ruth Rendell
thrillers	☐	Dick Francis, Alistair Maclean
spy stories	☐	John le Carré, Ian Fleming
historical novels	☐	Georgette Heyer, Ellis Peters
family sagas	☐	Howard Spring, Claire Rayner
short stories	☐	Saki, Frank O'Connor
modern plays	☐	Peter Nichols, Alan Ayckbourn
travel accounts	☐	Paul Theroux, Eric Newby
cookery books	☐	Jane Grigson, Delia Smith
popular science	☐	Desmond Morris, Steve Jones
translations from other languages	☐	Isabel Allende, Albert Camus
books about society	☐	Anthony Sampson, Jeremy Paxman
stories of films	☐	any popular film

2 Beside each of the boxes above, there is an example of the genre itself or of a writer who specialises in this field in English. Discuss these questions.

a Has anyone in the class read anything by any of the named authors? If so, what did they think of their work?

b Can anyone in the class suggest any other examples of each of the genres which other students in the class might enjoy? Note down any suggestions and keep the list to refer to in the future when you may want to find something to read in English.

Reading: Blurbs

Here are examples of the blurbs from four English works of fiction which you might enjoy. Think about these questions.

a In each case would the blurb tempt you to read the book or not?
b What was it about the blurb that either makes you feel you might like to read the book or else puts you off?

Vikram Seth's novel is, at its core, a love story: the tale of Lata's – and her mother's – attempts to find a suitable boy, through love or through exacting maternal appraisal. At the same time it is the story of India, newly independent and struggling through a time of crisis as a sixth of the world's population faces its first great General Election and the chance to map its own destiny.

'This novel, so vast and so amiably peopled, is a long, sweet, sleepless pilgrimage to life … Such writing reminds us that there are secrets beyond technique, beyond even style, which have to do with a quality of soul on the part of the writer, a giving of oneself … His novel deserves thousands of long marriages and suitable readers.'

James Wood, *Guardian*

'This may prove to be the most fecund as well as the most prodigious work of the latter half of the century – perhaps even the book to restore the serious reading public's faith in the contemporary novel … You should make time for it. It will keep you company for the rest of your life.'

Daniel Johnson, *The Times*

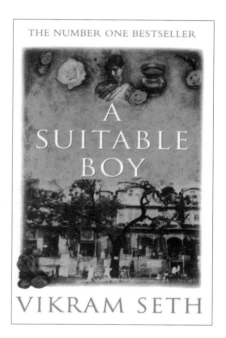

*Celebrate the season
with spirits of a creepier kind …*

Stoke the fire, fill your glass and prepare yourself for an evening of stories from the impressive collection of authors who have turned their hand to the supernatural.

A touch of wit from Charles Dickens as Mr Wardle recounts the mysterious disappearance of Gabriel Grub; a pistol-wielding ghoul from the pen of J M Barrie; the shadowy figure of a tall gentleman in a tale from the vivid imagination of L P Hartley. These are just a few of the spine-tingling classics, from the historical to the present day, with which to while away the winter hours.

The perfect present for those who yearn for a little extra seasonal shiver.

'I defy anyone to read Le Fanu's opening paragraph and not continue with the story.'
Scottish Field

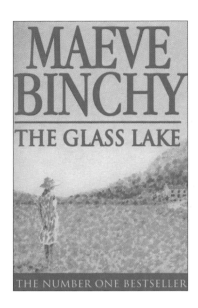

To the outsider, Kit McMahon growing up in the lakeside village of Lough Glass leads a charmed life. She is the loved daughter of Martin McMahon, the kindly local pharmacist and Helen, his beautiful wife. She has a little brother Emmet, a best friend Clio, and a host of other friends.

But all is not as it seems. Kit worries about her mother. Helen McMahon does not fit in with the people and the ways of Lough Glass. She wanders alone by the lake night after night – until the dark windy night when she disappears and only the lake knows the real reason.

This is the story of how Kit McMahon carries out her mother's last wishes; a story of how faith and courage can be rewarded. It is Maeve Binchy at her spellbinding best, creating a novel of such warmth and honour that the reader will never want it to end.

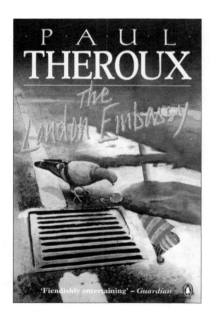

Sparkling metropolitan entertainment with Paul Theroux

Hero of *The Consul's File*, Theroux's diplomat has now been promoted and posted to London. In these episodes from his career – dinner with Mrs Thatcher, meeting a Russian defector, gossip, love affairs – he infiltrates the public lives and private events of the capital's rich and famous and, in doing so, draws us a new map of London.

'Fiendishly entertaining' – *Guardian*

'An alert, elegant, cunning book' – *Observer*

'Paul Theroux is a Somerset Maugham at heart, telling a story, conveying an atmosphere, getting an emotion dead right' – *Sunday Express*

Vocabulary: Language of publicity

When publicising a book in a blurb or in an advertisement of some other kind, publishers inevitably want to create a good impression of their book; they want to attract readers, to intrigue and impress them. Clearly, part of the way they do this is by using words that will make their work sound attractive. Here are some phrases from each of the reviews above which help to do this.

the most prodigious work of the latter half of the century

the perfect present

Maeve Binchy at her spellbinding best

Sparkling, metropolitan entertainment

1 Read through the reviews again and choose one other phrase from each of them which for you is a good example of the vocabulary of blurb writing.

Compare the phrases you chose with those selected by other students.

2 Here are some more extracts from blurbs, which use language characteristic of such publicity material.

This novel embodies the very best of R S
A compelling read
You won't be able to put it down!
An enthralling first novel by a writer who will soon
  be a household name
Shortlisted for the 1996 Booker Prize
An absolute must for romantics
A brilliant examination of the power of parental love
A gripping mystery

Take each of the above extracts and replace one or more words in each of them in order to make another phrase for a blurb. For example, you could modify the first one to:

This novel typifies the very best of R S
or
This novel embodies R S at her stunning best
or
This anthology embodies the very best of R S
and so on.

3 Follow these instructions.

1 If possible, find some examples of English books with blurbs on them – in a library or a bookshop, perhaps. Note down any phrases that you think could be useful for blurb-writing. Try to find four good phrases.
2 Compare the phrases you found with those collected by other students.
3 In pairs, write a blurb for this book – or any other you have been using on your English course. Use as much of the language practised in this section as possible. Remember that blurb-writers are interested in selling rather than telling the precise truth and nothing but the truth.

Grammar: Prepositions

1 Even the most advanced students usually need practice with prepositions. Here are the opening two paragraphs from *Wolverden Tower*, one of the *Ghosts for Christmas* stories, in which we meet the main characters in the story. Some prepositions have been omitted from the text. Can you find where they need to go and replace them?

> Maisie Llewelyn had not been invited Wolverden before; therefore she was not a little elated Mrs West's invitation. For Wolverden Hall, one the loveliest Elizabethan manor houses Kent, had been bought and fitted appropriate style (the phrase is the upholsterer's) Colonel West, the famous millionaire South Australia. The Colonel had lavished it untold wealth, fleeced the backs ten thousand sheep and an equal number his fellow-countrymen and Wolverden was now, if not the most beautiful, least the most opulent country-house easy reach London.
>
> Mrs West was waiting the station to meet Maisie. The house was full Christmas guests already, it is true, but Mrs West was a model stately old-fashioned courtesy: she would not have omitted meeting one the number any less excuse than a royal command to appear Windsor. She kissed Maisie both cheeks – she had always been fond Maisie – and sallied her the door the obsequious carriage.

2 Work with a partner.

1 Choose a text in English. It would be useful revision to use a text you worked on earlier in this book but you might also prefer to choose a text from another source.

2 Write the text out without any prepositions, as in the previous exercise.

3 Exchange texts with another pair. Can you complete each other's texts?

Listening: Describing character

⊡ **Listen to what the speaker on the tape says about presenting characters when writing a novel. Answer these questions.**

a What are the main points which the speaker is making?
b What kind of people is the speaker addressing?
c Do you think the points made are sound? Why (not)?

Note down five or six phrases used by the speaker which you particularly liked or which seem particularly significant for you. Compare the phrases you chose with those selected by other students. Why did you each choose your particular phrases?

Writing: Presenting characters

Here are some short extracts from each of the books whose blurbs you studied above. They all come from the beginning of the story in question and each extract is introducing a new character in the story for the first time. Read the extracts and then do the exercises which follow.

A

'You too will marry a boy I choose,' said Mrs Rapa Mehra firmly to her younger daughter.

Lata avoided the maternal imperative by looking around the great lamp-lit garden of Prem Nivas. The wedding-guests were gathered on the lawn. 'Hmm,' she said. This annoyed her mother further.

'I know what your hmms mean, young lady, and I can tell you I will not stand for hmms in this matter. I do know what is best. I am doing it all for you. Do you think it is easy for me, trying to arrange things for all four of my children without His help?' Her nose began to redden at the thought of her husband, who would, she felt certain, be partaking of their present joy from somewhere benevolently above.

B

The second Mrs Ryder was a young woman not easily frightened, but now she stood in the dusk of the passage leaning back against the wall, her hand on her heart, looking at the grey-faced window beyond which the snow was steadily falling against the lamplight.

The passage where she was led from the study to the dining-room, and the window looked out onto the little paved path that ran at the edge of the Cathedral green. As she stared down the passage, she couldn't be sure whether the woman was there or not. How absurd of her. She knew the woman was not there.

C

> With a shock Kit saw a figure through the window. Her mother was sitting at the table perfectly still. There was a faraway look on her face. She hadn't heard Kit, nor did she seem even aware of her surroundings. To Kit's dismay she saw that tears were falling down her mother's face and she wasn't even bothering to wipe them.

D

> Vic Scadato – 'Skiddoo' to the office – all gestures, all heel-clicks on the corridor tiles, shooting his pink cuffs, tugging at his earlobe, pinching his face at his reflection in the elevator mirror, tap-dancing as he talked and as his bubblegum snapped, saying, 'The Royal facility in Kensington has a really spacious function room,' then interrupting himself with 'I've got a stack of cables waiting' and 'I'm one of those rare people who has a nose for detail,' neighing his hideous laugh – 'It's my Italian blood,' he explained, and he was never breathless. He had teeth like piano keys and spit flew out of his mouth when he talked.

1 Match the adjectives to the characters.

Mrs Rapa Mehra   vain
Mrs Ryder   sensible
Kit's mother   distraught
Vic Scadato   alarmed
     garrulous
     self-pitying
     unattractive
     determined
     fidgety

2 Look again at the text used in the prepositions exercise on page 153. What do you learn there about the characters of Maisie, the Colonel and Mrs West?

3 In text D, the author could perhaps simply have said that Vic was 'a very vain person' but instead chooses to tell the reader this in a more indirect way.

How does the writer in each case indicate that the person has the characteristics identified in Exercises 1 and 2?

Do you think the techniques used to indicate character are more or less effective than a simple statement of what the person was like? Why?

4 Choose a novel and look at how the writer presents his or her characters. Can you find examples of the following?

– using dialogue to present character in a particularly effective way
– using a person's mannerisms or actions effectively to convey character or mood
– using description of a person's physical appearance to indicate character
– direct statement of what someone's character is like
– telling the reader about a person's thoughts
– describing something a person has done in order to suggest their character
– describing the person through the eyes of another, better known, person in the book
– any other striking methods of presenting character

The novel that you choose to look at may be in English or in any other language but you should be able to talk about the methods used, giving examples, in English.

Work in groups of three or four students. Share some of your most interesting insights and examples.

5 Choose one of the situations below to write about. Pay particular attention to at least one of the protagonists in the situation (the other might be you yourself, if you wish). Use your imagination and some of the techniques you have been talking about to present your character(s) to your readers.

– an old person is talking to his or her grandchild
– a couple meet for the first time and fall in love
– two old schoolfriends bump into each other after thirty years
– the first day at school for a new teacher or a new class
– two strangers meet on a train or plane

6 Exchange what you wrote in Exercise 5 with a partner. Read your partner's work and then note down for your partner:

a what techniques you think he or she has used to portray the person/people in his or her description
b what characteristics you feel the techniques indicate about the person
c whether you feel anything is not clear about the writing
d what else you would like to know about the person/people, i.e. what you feel could be appropriately added to the description
e what other ideas you may have for making the writing more effective

Read what your partner has written about your work. Make any alterations or additions that your partner suggests that you agree will improve your work.

The main aspects of language worked on in this unit are:

- understanding different accents
- American English
- reading – varieties of English
- flexible parts of speech
- varieties in vocabulary
- assessing your own progress

Warm-up: Varieties of English

There are many different ways of speaking English. Different areas have their own accents and, to some extent, their own vocabulary and occasionally their own differences as far as grammar is concerned. The best-known contrast, perhaps, is between British English and American English but important varieties of English are spoken in other countries as well – Ireland, Australia, India and South Africa, for example.

Even within Britain, every area has its own way of speaking. It is not really a matter of someone having, say, a Scottish accent – they have a Glasgow accent or an Edinburgh accent or an Aberdeen accent, for example. The phonetics professor in Bernard Shaw's play *Pygmalion* (made into the musical *My Fair Lady*) claimed that 'I can place any man within six miles. I can place him within two miles in London. Sometimes within two streets.' Increased mobility and mass communications have tended to make local accents less distinctive than they were in Professor Higgins' day but they are far from disappearing.

1 Discuss with two or three other students.

a Does everyone who speaks your language speak it in exactly the same way? If not, how do the different styles vary – in accent, vocabulary or grammar or a combination of these? Give examples if you can.

b Does a person's style of speech depend simply on where they come from or is it also a matter of class and/or educational level?

c Is any one style of speaking your language more prestigious than any other style? If so, which style? How do people feel about any other style(s) of speaking the language?

d Do you think people are beginning to use one particular style of speech more than any other nowadays? If so, which style and why are the changes occurring?

2 Now look at the questions in Exercise 1 again. Imagine that they were being answered by a group of native English speakers. How might they answer each of the questions?

Listening: Accents

1 ▱ Listen to these examples of people with different accents speaking English. The people here come from New Zealand, Scotland, the USA and Ireland, but not in that order. Answer these questions about each text.

a Who do you think is talking?
b What are they talking about?

2 ▱ Now listen again. As you listen, try to complete the table about the speakers.

	Characteristics of the accent – sounds, intonation etc.	Any other comments on the style of speaking (for example, vocabulary or grammar used)	Geographical origin of accent
1			
2			
3			
4			

The next few exercises deal with the American variety of English, which was commented on by one of the speakers on the tape. Note that few of the answers can be found on the tape.

3 Discuss whether the following general statements are true or false. Where possible, give examples to illustrate the truth or otherwise of the statement.

a American spelling is often simpler than British spelling.

b There are words which have one meaning in British English and a completely different meaning in American English.

c The British tend to be stricter about grammar rules than the Americans.

d American English makes much more use of the present perfect tense than British English does.

e American English uses a number of words and expressions that were common in British English but are no longer used in the UK.

f American slang is more lively and varied than British slang.

g American pronunciation is easier to understand than British English.

h A British accent is highly valued in the USA.

i Americans are more likely to understand a British person speaking English than vice versa.

4 Here are a number of words which cause particular confusion as they can have different meanings in British and American English. Explain what the two different meanings are.

1 a billion
2 a professor
3 a purse
4 chips

5 pants
6 gas
7 school
8 the first floor

9 to wash up
10 biscuit
11 jelly
12 vest

5 Here are some more examples of differences between American and British vocabulary. Can you match the American word on the left with its British equivalent on the right?

buffet	face flannel
can	bumper
candy	estate agent
closet	estate car
diaper	sideboard
drug store	cupboard
eggplant	power point
elevator	tap
faucet	chemist
fender	drawing pin
outlet	nappy
realtor	braces
sidewalk	boot
station wagon	tin
suspenders	windscreen
thumbtack	spanner
traffic circle	lift
trunk (car)	aubergine
washcloth	sweets
windshield	roundabout
wrench	pavement

6 How many other examples of American vocabulary that is different from British vocabulary can you and a partner write down in two minutes?

Compare your lists with those of other pairs. Which pair thought of most words? How many words did the class think of as a whole?

7 Here are some examples of language that is more typically American than British from the point of view of grammar. What would a British person be more likely to say?

a Bill arrived at five after eight.
b The movie was real good.
c I snuck quietly out of the theater.
d I'll go get the book.
e I'll be here Monday through Friday.
f I didn't see it yet.
g John is meeting with him tomorrow.
h You've gotten off lightly this time.

Reading: Varieties of English

1 Just as varieties of the spoken language are distinct, so are varieties of the written language. Here it is not a matter of the speaker's place of origin being identifiable but of where the text came from, i.e. from a novel, an engineering textbook, a newspaper article, etc. Most native speakers would be able to look at the extracts below and say what kind of writing they came from. Can you do the same? In each case, say what type of text the extract comes from and explain how you were able to deduce this.

A

See the wealth of colour of the flowers in the window boxes, the white crests to the waves lapping on the shore, the familiar livery of the lifeboat. All of these intricate details have been expertly painted by hand to create a sculpture of exceptional quality.

What's more, each piece is impressed with Jane Hart's signature and accompanied by a serially-numbered certificate – your guarantee of authenticity.

B

Start by creaming the butter and sugar together until they're light, clean and fluffy. Beat the egg yolks thoroughly together and add them to the mixture about a teaspoonful at a time, beating well after each addition. When all the yolks are in, lightly fold in the ground almonds, grated chocolate and milk, using a metal spoon.

C

Blessed are the poor in spirit: for theirs is the kingdom of heaven.
Blessed are they that mourn: for they shall be comforted.
Blessed are the meek: for they shall inherit the earth.
Blessed are they which do hunger and thirst after righteousness: for they shall be filled.

D

Subject to the above paragraph, no person receiving a copy of this letter in any territory other than the United Kingdom may treat the same as constituting an invitation to her/him unless in the relevant territory such an invitation could lawfully be made to her/him without compliance with any registration or other legal requirements. It is the responsibility of any person outside the United Kingdom wishing to elect to receive new ordinary shares in the company to satisfy herself/himself as to full observance of the laws of the relevant territory in connection therewith, including obtaining any governmental or other consents which may be required and observing any other formalities needing to be observed in such territory.

E

Work in M st patt to match Back at the same time inc 1 st at each end of the 7th and every foll 14th row until there are 79 (**81**:81:**93**:85) sts. Work straight until Sleeve measures 42 (**43**:44:**44**:45)cm from cast-on edge, ending after a WS row.

F

The illustration on the facing page shows all the equipment you will need to set up your system and begin using it. Set up your equipment on a sturdy surface near a grounded wall outlet. Before following the set-up instructions in this chapter, you may want to read 'Arranging Your Office' in Appendix A (in the section on health-related information) for tips on adjusting your work furniture so that you're comfortable when using your Macintosh.

2 Now do some group work on the vocabulary of these texts.

1 Work in five or six groups. Each group should take one of the above texts and should underline all the words and expressions in it which are clues as to the origin of the text. Make sure that you could explain what each of the underlined words and expressions means to other students in the class.
2 Tell the class as a whole which words you underlined and explain the meanings of any words or expressions which any other student asks you to explain.

Vocabulary: Varieties in vocabulary

The vocabulary of the extracts above was a clue to the type of text they came from. Here we are going to look at some particular aspects of vocabulary relating to the fields exemplified by the above six extracts.

1 Technology – indeed contemporary society in general – regularly needs to invent new words. Affixes are used quite frequently when new words are being formed. The affix *cyber*, for example, is frequently used to mean 'electronic' as in such current coinages as 'cyberspace' and 'cybertalk'.

You probably won't be able to find the underlined words in these sentences in your dictionary but use both the context and what you know about the meaning of their constituent parts (prefix, root, suffix) to make a guess at what the word probably means.

a Teleworking is becoming more and more frequent these days with improved and cheaper technology.
b New shampoos claim to have added a volumiser so that they can make your hair look even more attractive.
c An autonumerologist, interviewed in the newspaper today, says that there are two main types of popular plates.
d There has been talk of replacing the breathalyser with an eyelyser.
e Ecotourism is the latest trend in holiday-making.
f Jane is a clothesaholic. She spends all her spare cash on things that I'm sure she hardly ever wears.
g A year ago *The Guardian* was rash enough to refer to a new nadir in our cricketing fortunes. Rarely in the long history of nadirology can there have been a less judicious assessment. (*The Guardian*, 16 August 1989)

h Both mergerites and anti-mergerites hurried forward to claim their share of the blame, knowing that nothing in British politics succeeds like apology. (*Daily Telegraph*, 4 September 1987)

2 Many words of the type used in Exercise 1 will not have a very long life. They are merely coined by journalists sometimes for humorous effect and sometimes to describe something that is a new phenomenon or concept in society. It can be fun to try your hand at inventing words too.

Here are the definitions of some more words which have been recently coined. Using what you know about prefixes and suffixes, can you suggest what the word might be?

a someone who is addicted to chocolates
b prejudice against people who are much bigger or much smaller than the average
c a little house in the country where teleworkers live and work
d a person who has been electronically tagged (e.g. so that the police are always aware of where they are)
e an irresistible urge to collect things

3 🔊 Listen to the speaker talking about the coining of new words in English. Answer these questions.

a What words does she refer to and what do they mean?
b What general points is she making about the coining of new words?

4 Advertising language is characterised by its use of positive and attractive-sounding adjectives. A survey has been carried out into which adjectives are most frequently used in adverts. The most common was 'new' and number 20 was 'rich'. Suggest what the five or six of the others might have been.

A richer blend of coffee

The newest technology so you can keep in touch

Rich colours for a new woman

newer, smaller, better

It's New, It's **Blue**, It's You.

The *richest* selection

5 Follow these instructions.

1 Choose a product or a service, e.g. a car, a brand of cosmetics, a hotel, a college or a language course.

2 In pairs, write an advert for the product or service chosen by the class using as many as possible of the 20 adjectives in Exercise 4.

3 Compare the adverts written by different students in the class. Which do you think is most effective?

Grammar: Flexible parts of speech

The English language is very flexible in that many nouns frequently take the role of adjectives and even verbs. You heard the newscaster, for example, talk about someone being *sidelined* (from the expression *on the sidelines*, meaning not in a position to influence anyone).

1 Underline all the examples of nouns used as verbs which you can find in the text below. Find a synonym for each of these nouns and, if possible, explain what the connection is between the meaning of the noun and how it is used as a verb. Note that many of the nouns used as verbs in this way are quite colloquial; they are used metaphorically to create – originally at least – quite a strong image.

THE JOURNALIST was anxious to ferret out the truth behind a rumour he had heard about the Prime Minister. He was said to be feathering his own nest on the strength of some government decisions. The journalist knew he had to get to Edinburgh where a party was being hosted that evening for top party officials. He didn't want to fork out for his fare to Scotland and so he thumbed a lift in a lorry. There were terrible traffic jams on the way north and the lorry could only inch its way forward. Finally, they reached Edinburgh and the journalist elbowed his way past security guards, flashing his press pass. He buttonholed an MP famed for his indiscretion and egged him on to talk about the rumours. It was clear that the PM was not toeing the line and the journalist soon had a story ready to fax to his paper.

2 In pairs, find three or four more examples of the following.

a parts of the body used as verbs as well as nouns
b animals used as verbs as well as nouns
c foodstuffs used as verbs as well as nouns
d people or professions used as verbs as well as nouns
e items of furniture or household objects used as verbs as well as nouns

3 Note also how easy it is for nouns to be used adjectivally in English as in, for example, *a table lamp, a shoe shop, head office, a mystery man, a tennis ball* and so on.

In pairs, think of two or three different nouns which you could use to complete each of these sentences.

a Meg has bought some beautiful new .... shoes.
b The town where we live is a .... town.
c I'd hate to work in a .... shop.
d Would you like to try the .... soup followed by the .... salad?
e Her boyfriend works in a .... company.
f Please buy me a .... book as a .... present.

4 Just as nouns can be used as verbs, so some prepositions are occasionally used as adjectives or verbs.

In all of the sentences below, the blanks can be filled by a word or expression which is normally a preposition but here has a different function. Can you fill the blanks and explain what the word means in each case? The first one has been done for you as an example. Notice that most of these sentences are very colloquial.

> afters   down   down and outs   in
> ins and outs   off   on and off   out   over
> up   up and down

a It is very important for some teenagers to be wearing the <u>in</u> clothes.
(*In* is used here as an adjective and means in the latest fashion of the peer group.)
b There's a rumour that they're going to .... the price of petrol in the next election.
c Theirs is an .... relationship whereas ours is a rather .... one.
d I don't really understand all the .... of the situation. Could you explain them to me?
e There are far more .... in the centre of London than there used to be twenty years ago.
f Have you seen how fast he can .... a glass of beer?
g I believe there are six balls in one .... in cricket.
h Everybody has their .... days, don't they?
i Is there anything for ....?

Speaking: In the style of ...

Unless you are planning a career on the stage, you probably do not need to practise speaking in different English accents. But it may help you to extend your range of English-speaking skills if you practise speaking in the styles of different professionals and types of people.

1 Here are some types of people and some topics for conversations.

Check that you know the meanings of everything on the lists.

> anarchist   banker   computer enthusiast   cook   doctor
> hypochondriac   keep fit fanatic   lawyer   misogynist
> optimist   pessimist   poet   police officer   psychiatrist
> school teacher   vicar

> books   TV programme   lunch   weekend plans   marriage
> the government   last night   last holiday   life   love   pets
> weather

2 Follow these instructions.

1 As a class, add four or more words or phrases to each of the lists in Exercise 1.

2 Discuss in twos or threes what you feel will be the special speech characteristics of each of the people in the first list and how this might influence the way they would talk about any one of the topics in the second list.

3 Now you are ready to play the game.

1 Divide into two teams.

2 The teacher will give each person in each team a character chosen at random from the list. Do not tell anyone who your character is. The teacher then announces a topic and each person must decide how their character would talk about this topic.

3 In turns, pairs of students – one from each team – come to the front to act out their characters' conversation on that topic.

4 After one to two minutes the conversation stops and each team has three chances to guess who their team member's character was.

If they identify the character in their first guess, then their team gets five points, if on their second guess three points and if on their third guess one point. If they do not get it right on their third guess, then the other team gets three points.

Study skills: Assessing your own progress

It can be an interesting and useful exercise to see how your perception of your own progress compares with that of your fellow-students and your teacher.

Before you do the exercises below, look back at work that you did when you were at the beginning of this book. If possible, listen to the recording that you made when you did the Study skills exercise in Unit 1.

1 Discuss with other students.

a What have you particularly enjoyed about this course?

b In which areas of language learning, e.g. reading, writing, speaking, listening, grammar, vocabulary, do you feel you have learnt most during this course?

c Do you intend now just to try to keep up your level of English or do you want to go on learning a lot more?

d How do you intend to either keep up or learn more English?

2 Fill in the table below about your work and the progress you have made.

	Progress made during the course on a scale from 1 to 5 (1 = a little and 5 = a lot)	Where I feel this aspect of my English now is on a 1 to 5 scale (1 = not nearly good enough and 5 = good enough for all my needs)	Areas I still need to work on
reading			
writing			
listening			
speaking			
grammar/accuracy			
vocabulary			

Compare the marks and comments you wrote about yourself with those which your teacher gives you.

3 Take a blank piece of paper and write a list of the names of the students in the class down the left-hand side of the sheet. Beside each name write a sentence that describes something that strikes you as particularly positive about that person's performance in English. For example:

Noriko is very good at explaining what words mean.
Maria's pronunciation is excellent.
Ahmed has an enormous vocabulary.
Jan is good at telling jokes in English.

When everyone is ready, pass round all the sheets and read what everyone has written about you.

Tapescripts

Unit 1 Listening Exercise 1

ANNOUNCER: Helen Sharman is another woman who has won a place in history as Britain's first astronaut. I don't think my colleague, John Tidmarsh, has any plans to follow Helen into space but he certainly wanted to know how she set about getting herself into orbit.

HELEN SHARMAN: I was driving my car home from work, I was trying to listen to some music really, I was just flicking through the radio stations, finding some light music or something when an advert caught my attention rather than the music. And the advert went: Astronaut wanted, no experience necessary. And then went on to describe that the Soviets had offered the opportunity to somebody from the United Kingdom to train and then to blast off on one of their rockets and to do experiments in space. I thought wow, yes, this is something I really want to do because I had never thought about being an astronaut before that. I mean, nobody tells you at school that if you study sciences and keep up with your languages, then maybe one day you can be an astronaut.

JOHN TIDMARSH: It was an immediate decision in fact, was it?

HELEN SHARMAN: Absolutely. I mean I was, I did chemistry at university. I'd been an engineer and then a technologist and I enjoyed my job very much. I'd never thought about being an astronaut. There was never the opportunity for anybody from this country to be an astronaut. Now maybe if I'd grown up in Russia or America, maybe that would have been an ambition, but there was no chance as far as I was concerned when I was a child.

JOHN TIDMARSH: You had some of the some of the right qualifications they'd been looking for, though?

HELEN SHARMAN: They wanted a scientist or technologist, primarily, and the job was to do experiments in space. I mean that was the prime job. And of course the training and the launch and the weightlessness and looking back at the earth, all of those things are extras. The actual job was to do experiments in space so, yes, we had to be scientists.

JOHN TIDMARSH: Also it had to be someone who was extremely fit even before you went through their programme. I mean, were you a sportswoman?

HELEN SHARMAN: Yes, we had to be, like, internally healthy and already of a certain standard of fitness. But really, I mean, I love swimming and cycling and running that kind of fitness the aerobic stuff and of course what the Russians wanted to train me to do was to have big muscles. I had to be very strong. I put on three kilos over my shoulders and arms, really, so that I could operate effectively in a space suit. It was a different kind of thing than I was used to, a different kind of fitness. I mean, it's no good having somebody who likes to run marathons on board a space station, you can't go very far.

JOHN TIDMARSH: Thirteen thousand people applied for this job.

HELEN SHARMAN: Yes, initially of course I had no idea when I applied how many other people would also apply but when I discovered that 13,000 others also had applied I thought that I just didn't stand a chance. I really was in two minds whether I should just pull out and forget the whole thing but something made me just keep on going.

Unit 1 Listening Exercise 2

JOHN TIDMARSH: What about the moment when you knew you were the one who had been selected?

HELEN SHARMAN: I don't think I ever really believed it would be me until the day of the launch when not only had I put on my spacesuit and I'd climbed inside that rocket but I was sitting up there, the checks had been done and twenty minutes before the launch they turn on these emergency rockets because at that stage if there's a fire on the launch pad there is no time to unstrap from the seats and climb out of the rocket, get down in the lift and get away from the danger. So the emergency rockets literally pull away the small capsules on top of this rocket with its occupants – there were three of us – and they pull us away two kilometres down the road, hopefully to safety. Now when those rockets were turned on, that's when I knew that I was going up somehow.

JOHN TIDMARSH: What a moment it must be though as the launch takes place.

HELEN SHARMAN: It's really quite strange because it's such a relief, all of the training and the build-up to the launch and the two weeks of quarantine and then going through all the final checks. When it really is the launch time there is so much to do and to take account of that it's just a relief to be doing something that you've been training to do for so long and it's something, a fantastic togetherness feeling, we were doing it together, our crew and we were going to make this a success. I never ever believed that I would die and I don't think any of us did.

JOHN TIDMARSH: Your first thoughts when you saw the incredible view?

HELEN SHARMAN: The blueness of it, the brilliant white clouds and the brick-red deserts, we could see roads, you know anything that's long and straight and then when we went over into the darkness we could see the lights from cities, fires burning in Kuwait because when I flew a year ago it was the end of the Gulf War.

JOHN TIDMARSH: The space station. What did you do when you were there? What was your scientific programme?

HELEN SHARMAN: Well, it was to do many experiments ranging from medical experiments where I took for instance samples of blood and I analysed all the different constituents of my blood right through to growing crystals, and geophysics things actually, sort of taking measurements of the surface of the earth, measuring even things like the colour because that can give us such a lot of information about how much salt there is in that part of the world, how much water, what vegetation grows there and so for uninhabited areas it's very very useful. So I did a whole range of things, and things that you just can't do on earth, fascinating, especially for a scientist.

Unit 1 Listening Exercise 3

JOHN TIDMARSH: I'm told you didn't want to come back.

HELEN SHARMAN: I didn't want to come back and there is just really so many things to do. I'd been in space in total for only eight days, the novelty was still there, there was so much to do and of course the people who I was with they were really my best friends by then.

JOHN TIDMARSH: The return journey, there must be a touch of anxiety about that, though?

HELEN SHARMAN: The return journey, we always know is more dangerous than the launch and it's physically harder but it was a fantastic thing coming back. Because as you come through the surface of the atmosphere the air around us because we're going so fast is very hot and forms a thin layer of very hot air a plasma around the side of the spacecraft which has the most gorgeous colours, I mean, browns and oranges and yellows, but no it *is* physically harder. I felt as though my

ribs were crushing my lungs. Because coming back in through the atmosphere I was four and a half times heavier than normal on earth, so my ribs were four and a half times heavier, it was difficult to breathe and of course you are all the time waiting for this big bump when you actually hit the ground.

JOHN TIDMARSH: Hoping the parachutes have opened.

HELEN SHARMAN: Well, you know when the parachutes have opened there's a severe jostling.

JOHN TIDMARSH: That must be a good moment, yes. You came down in where Kazakhstan, was it?

HELEN SHARMAN: In Northern Kazakhstan, that's right, in the desert.

JOHN TIDMARSH: What about all these comrades of yours, are you still in touch with them?

HELEN SHARMAN: Yes, they're my friends, they're my colleagues, and I will never ever forget them. I was over in, in Russia and Kazakhstan I saw a launch of the next supply ship that was going up. Every two months they have another supply ship going to the station with more experiments and more food and oxygen supplies and I was able to plant a tree down at the launch site. Every person who flies plants a tree, so Gagarin of course the first person ever to fly into space, his tree is a good 40 feet high by now. My tree is one of the smaller ones at the very end of this long line of cosmonauts.

JOHN TIDMARSH: But growing well and well watered?

HELEN SHARMAN: I hope so. The soldiers promised me that they would water it.

Unit 5 Listening Exercise 2

CHAIRPERSON: Clement Freud, your turn to begin. What to do with the hole in the doughnut. That is the subject that Ian Messiter has thought of for you and so can you talk about what to do with the hole in the doughnut for 60 seconds, starting now?

CLEMENT FREUD: It's pretty difficult to spend sixty seconds on discussing what to do with the hole in the doughnut because when you have said fill it, it is left only to discuss the methods of filling and the means whereby this could be effected. Jam is a very popular substance but lemon curd or even cream has been known to be inserted into the midst of this mass of pastry before it is sugared and fried in deep fat. In the army where people …

CHAIRPERSON: Peter Jones has challenged. Why?

PETER JONES: Well, it isn't made of pastry. It's made of dough. Doughnut. It's made of dough.

KENNETH WILLIAMS: Amazing, really, Clem left himself open there to that because he's supposed to be an expert, isn't he, on all this food business, (Exactly) you wouldn't have thought he'd have left himself open like that, would you?

CHAIRPERSON: It's probably classified as a pastry but I think we give it to him because of the dough, don't you, Clement?

CLEMENT FREUD: Yes.

CHAIRPERSON: Good. 30 seconds on what to do with the hole in the doughnut, Peter Jones, starting now.

PETER JONES: Well, of course, quite apart from filling it with cream, flavoured or otherwise, you can peer through it at a number of things.

CHAIRPERSON: Clement Freud has challenged. Why?

CLEMENT FREUD: Deviation. You really can't.

CHAIRPERSON: Well, if you lift a doughnut up to your eye, you can peer through it because it's got a large hole.

CLEMENT FREUD: No, it doesn't come out the other side.

CHAIRPERSON: Oh yes, you are thinking, you forget the round doughnuts that have a hole that go right through them, you can put them on your finger.

KENNETH WILLIAMS: No, no, no, (That is not a doughnut) that is not a doughnut, that is a doughnut ring which is quite another thing.

CHAIRPERSON: It's still a doughnut. 'It's not a doughnut, it's a doughnut ring'! Well, if it's not a doughnut, what is it?

KENNETH WILLIAMS: I'm afraid, no, I'm afraid Clement is quite right. The hole in the doughnut, that has got nothing to do with doughnut rings.

CHAIRPERSON: I think Kenneth put it perfectly well … Shut up, Kenneth … when he said it's not a doughnut, it's a doughnut ring. Peter Jones, you keep the subject and there are 20 seconds on what to do with a hole in the doughnut starting now.

PETER JONES: You can thread raffia through a number of holes …

CHAIRPERSON: Kenneth Williams has challenged.

KENNETH WILLIAMS: There is no question about this. Nobody would go round putting raffia through doughnuts. I've never heard such utter rubbish in my life. (Kenneth) You earlier on accused a member of this team of talking balderdash. You stood there and said it, sat there actually.

CHAIRPERSON: I didn't say anything. Peter Jones said it. Now listen, if you wanted to put a bit of raffia through a hole in a doughnut, you have a wonderful party game there, holding it up and seeing who could bite the most out of it. Peter Jones, you have another point. And you have 17 seconds on what to do with the hole in the doughnut, starting now.

PETER JONES: And make a kind of necklace which can be decorative and be very handy if you …

CHAIRPERSON: Kenneth Williams has challenged.

KENNETH WILLIAMS: Deviation I've never seen anyone going around in … a doughnut necklace …

CHAIRPERSON: I've never seen anybody with a doughnut necklace but it's perfectly possible if you were kinky and …

KENNETH WILLIAMS: Right out of your own mouth, you have convicted yourself.

CHAIRPERSON: He has not deviated, he has not deviated from the subject on the card which is what to do with a hole in the doughnut. He has put raffia round it and he has put it round his neck. He can do what he likes with it providing he doesn't deviate from the subject. He has 11 seconds on what to do with the hole in the doughnut, Peter Jones, starting now.

PETER JONES: It can be extremely helpful if you feel like a nibble and want to eat something before you take it off.

CHAIRPERSON: Clement Freud has challenged. Why?

CLEMENT FREUD: Deviation.

CHAIRPERSON: Why?

CLEMENT FREUD: The one thing you can't nibble is the hole in the doughnut.

PETER JONES: I didn't, I didn't say you could eat the hole.

CHAIRPERSON: You did establish that, Peter.

PETER JONES: I said you make a necklace of the doughnuts and then you nibble the doughnuts.

KENNETH WILLIAMS: Don't try and wriggle out of it, mate, don't try …

CHAIRPERSON: The subject is what to do with the hole in the doughnut.

DEREK NIMMO: He's right.

PETER JONES: Derek Nimmo says I'm right.

CHAIRPERSON: Well, Derek Nimmo is against me entirely in so many ways. You were talking about, the subject is what to do with a hole in the doughnut and you talked about eating, so you were either deviating from the subject or else you were being devious …

PETER JONES: Well, naturally you eat the hole with the rest of the doughnut; it's not done to ignore the hole and leave it at the side of the plate.

CHAIRPERSON: All right, they've both chalked up metaphorical points for cleverness and rapport and wit. Clement Freud, he has a point for a correct challenge. What to do with a hole in the doughnut, Clement, four seconds starting now.

CLEMENT FREUD: In the Royal Navy, there was a directive …

CHAIRPERSON: Kenneth Williams has challenged.

KENNETH WILLIAMS: Deviation. The Royal Navy has nothing to do with doughnuts, they have rum.

CHAIRPERSON: He hadn't got going. He has two seconds left on what to do with a hole in the doughnut, starting now.

CLEMENT FREUD: Whereas the Air Force …

Unit 7 Listening Exercise 1

The first time I came to Europe was in 1972, skinny, shy, alone. In those days the only cheap flights were from New York to Luxembourg with a refuelling stop on route at Keflavik Airport near Reykjavik. The airplanes were old and engagingly past their prime. And they were achingly slow. It took a week and a half to reach Keflavik, a small grey airport in the middle of a flat grey nowhere, and another week and a half to bounce on through the skies to Luxembourg. Everyone on the plane was a hippie, except the crew and two herring factory executives in first class. It was rather like being on a Greyhound bus on the way to a folk-singers' convention.

The plane dropped out of the clouds and there below me was the sudden magical tableau of small green fields and steepled villages spread over an undulating landscape like a shaken out quilt that's settling back onto a bed. I had flown a lot in America but I'd never seen much of anything from any airplane window but endless golden fields on farms the size of Belgium, meandering rivers and pencil lines of black highway as straight as taut wire. It always looked vast and mostly empty. You felt that if you squinted hard enough you'd see all the way to Los Angeles even when you were over Kansas.

But here the landscape had the ordered perfection of a model railway layout. It was all so green and minutely cultivated, so compact, so tidy, so fetching, so European. I was smitten. I still am. It was all so different: the language, the money, the cars, the number plates on the cars, the bread, the food, the newspapers, the parks, the people. I'd never seen a zebra crossing before. Never seen a tram. Never seen an unsliced loaf of bread. Never even considered it an option. Never seen anyone wearing a beret who expected to be taken seriously. Never seen people go to a different shop for each item of dinner or provide their own shopping bags. Never seen feathered pheasants and unskinned rabbits hanging in a butcher's window or pigs' heads smiling on a platter. Never seen a packet of Gitanes or the Michelin Man. And the people. Why, they were Luxembourgers. I don't know why this amazed me so, but it did. I began thinking 'that man over there, he's a Luxembourger and so is that girl. They don't know anything about the New York Yankees. They don't know the theme tune to the Mickey Mouse Club. They're from another world.' It was just wonderful.

Unit 7 Speaking Exercise 4

Ladies and gentlemen, I have been invited here today to tell you about my trip across the Sahara on a camel. You may wonder why on earth a banker with a comfortable job in the City would want to leave his air-conditioned office and his executive lunches to head for the sweltering sands of the Sahara Desert. So let me begin by trying to explain why I decided to exchange my Porsche for a camel – temporarily, at least. It all began in the dentist's waiting room. Trying to distract myself from the noise of the drill which I could hear reminding me that it would soon be my turn, I picked up a copy of the *National Geographic* and was struck by some stunningly beautiful photographs of the rippling sands of the desert. I have brought along some of those photos today and I think that if you look at this one in particular you may begin to understand why I suddenly felt an intense longing to get away from the traffic jams, the fumes and the noise of London.

Unit 9 Listening Exercise 1

HOBDAY: And a very good morning to you all from Peter Hobday in London.

REDHEAD: And from Brian Redhead on the British Gas complex 25 miles off-shore here in the middle of Morecambe Bay. We have called this week 'Energy Week' on 'Today', National Energy Week even, and this morning we have come to British Gas in Morecambe Bay to talk to the Secretary of State for Energy, Mr Peter Walker, about the nation's energy policy. I arrived last night. Mr Walker arrived only a few minutes ago by helicopter. Good morning.

WALKER: Good morning, Brian.

REDHEAD: Have you been here before?

WALKER: I've been on many rigs but not this exciting new rig at British Gas. It really is, I think, very exciting to come out to this staggering development.

REDHEAD: Now this British Gas complex in Morecambe Bay is the latest energy source to come on stream, but in all the main energy businesses – coal, gas, oil, nuclear power – new things are happening or about to happen; coal in South Warwickshire, the ninth round of North Sea licences, Torness and perhaps Sizewell B. But we'll start here and I've been joined by Dr Harold Hughes, who's Director and General Manager of Exploration Companies and Cedric Browne, who's Director of the Morecambe Bay project. Dr Hughes, first. Everybody else was in the North Sea. How come you found gas in Morecambe Bay?

HUGHES: Originally another large multinational company was here. We got hold of their data after they had walked away as having pronounced themselves uninterested. We looked at the data, decided that they had misinterpreted it, found a very large structure here, drilled it and we have Morecambe Field, which is the country's largest, second largest gas field hold in UK waters.

REDHEAD: Well, now, I mean, did you find when you began to develop it that you could use exactly the same techniques as you used in the North Sea?

HUGHES: No, we found that with the different conditions in Morecambe Bay we needed to develop different ideas. There's a thirty-foot tidal variation here and, even though there's only a hundred foot of water, the thirty-foot tide, the rapid tidal rates meant we had to do some innovative designs. The slant drilling which is necessary to develop the field as well is the first time in European waters and that was quite a unique feature out here.

REDHEAD: Right now, having found it, devised a way of developing it and now that you're operating it, is it a simple, straightforward operation as it would be anywhere else or has it daily difficulties?

HUGHES: Well, I think I might want to say that nothing off-shore is simple and straightforward at any time. We have very much the same sort of equipment that you find in the North Sea. There's very little difference in principle between oil and gas rigs. This is a very large set-up, of course, because of the size of the field and it promises to get even larger in future years – one could envisage 11 or 12 platforms here eventually when we've finished developing.

REDHEAD: Now, have you found all the gas that's here or do you suspect there's some more?

HUGHES: We have other exploration blocks nearby. We have found two other small fields which we will hook into this field eventually but we don't think the potential of either our blocks or more particularly this general area is by any means over. We think there's a lot more gas in Morecambe Bay.

REDHEAD: Now, Mr Browne, if there's an awful lot of gas in Morecambe Bay, ought we not to leave it there for a while? Is it wise to be pumping it ashore and burning it up?

BROWNE: No, we need to bring it ashore, we've sixteen million customers. They have an appetite for gas in the winter months. The demand increases by a factor of five in the winter compared to the summer and we need to be prepared to meet that rapid increase in demand. And a field like Morecambe enables us to bring the gas on stream and effectively supply for the next forty years the whole of the Greater Manchester area.

REDHEAD: No better area to supply with gas. Now, what is then the future of gas in both Morecambe Bay and the North Sea? What amount of gas have you got in the nation's energy?

HUGHES: Oh, we have gas I'm sure which will last us well into the next century, till 2010, probably more so. The history of exploration around the world generally is that, as you develop new techniques, you find more reserves both of oil and gas. And I think we can look forward to successive new discoveries but, of course, one must say, that the fields will become smaller, statistically that's the expectation. And so we shall have to look harder, we shall have develop better techniques for finding the small fields and we shall have to learn how to develop those fields as economically as we can.

REDHEAD: Now, in doing that, do you see gas as being a fuel if we put a figure at ten years into the next century, perhaps twenty, is it possible that there will be natural gas around these islands for much longer?

BROWNE: I think there is. Erm. Certainly we expect to see the gas lasting into the twentieth year of the next century and beyond, and I think that more indications are there will be more reserves. We may have to go further out into deeper waters but I think around these islands there'll be sufficient to see us well into the next century and of really no concern to probably anybody who's listening to this programme at the moment.

REDHEAD: We'll all be dead before you've used up all the gas.

BROWNE: Well, I would imagine so.

REDHEAD: Now, one final question then, could it be that we don't even know how much we've got or is all the exploration over? We know what there is, we've just got to find and get it out.

HUGHES: Oh, by no means is all the exploration over. There's a great amount of work to be done, not only in this sea area but in other sea areas around the United Kingdom, the continental shelf.

REDHEAD: Well, Dr Hughes and Mr Browne, thank you both very much …

Unit 11 Listening Exercise 2

War, delegates, war has always been a confused affair, and in bygone days, commanders were taught that, when in doubt, when in doubt, they should march their troops towards the sound of gunfire. I intend to march my troops towards the sound of gunfire.

Politics are confused. And the fog of political controversy can obscure many issues, but we will march always towards the sound of the guns. Our government for too long has pretended not to see what it does not like. It has put its telescope to the blind eye in a very un-Nelsonian move. It puts its telescope to the blind eye so that it can say that there is no enemy in sight.

But, delegates, there are enemies. There are difficulties to be faced, there are decisions to be made, there is passion to be generated. The enemy is complacency and wrong values and inertia, inertia in the face of incompetence and injustice. It is against this enemy that we march.

We are not alone. The reforms that we advocate are inexorably written into the future. We move with the great trends of this century. Other nations have rebuilt their institutions under the hard discipline of war. It is for Liberals to show that Britain, proud Britain, can do this through a free people without passing through the furnace of defeat.

Unit 13 Listening Exercise 1

This little Italian boy when he was six years old presented a puzzle to people because he appeared blind in one eye. And yet the eye seemed perfectly normal and he as a child seemed perfectly normal. He didn't have any brain damage or anything like that. No one really understood why he was blind in one eye. And let's have a look at him here having his eyes tested. Here he is with a doctor doing extensive examinations on his eyes. A real mystery. Why should he be blind in just one eye when everything seemed normal? Well, the reason was – it was finally discovered on questioning the mother – that when he was very small, only a few weeks old, this eye, the eye that is now blind, had been bandaged just for a short but critical period of time and during that time, that was the critical time when the nerves were developing. As we can see on the next graphic, here is a scheme of the little boy's eyes. Here is the normal eye, making contact with its appropriate targets. And here is the eye that was blindfolded, which was bandaged, for a short period of time and during that period of time because the eye wasn't working the connections here were not established as they should be, and instead this eye, because nature abhors a vacuum, you won't have territory unclaimed, this immediately sent, this other eye, the good eye, the unbandaged eye, sent connections into the territory of the bandaged eye. So by the time the bandage was taken off and the neurone wanted to work, the eye wanted to work, it couldn't, no territory left available for it. Blind in one eye. So this shows that another factor in establishing neuronal connections is that neurones like to work, they have to work. The harder they work, the more firm the contacts. Otherwise the neurones will die.

Unit 15 Listening Exercises 1–3

MAX CARRADOS: Why did you come to me, Miss Whitmarsh?

MADELEINE: I'd heard of your wonderful powers. Shall I tell you how, does it matter?

MAX CARRADOS: Not in the least.

MADELEINE: I felt sure that you were the right man, but …

MAX CARRADOS: But?

MADELEINE: I really don't know where to start.

LAWYER: And now to the final provision.

FRANK: About time.

WILLIAM: Patience, brother. Not that you've anything to wait for.

FRANK: You bastard.

LAWYER: Gentlemen, please. Thank you. The final provision. And now to the passing on of the ancient Whitmarsh heritage, the lands that have been farmed by our family since the fifteenth century.

WILLIAM: Yes, yes, yes.

LAWYER: To my firstborn son, William junior … Please, sir … I bequeath exactly half of the family lands and holdings …

WILLIAM: Half, half!

LAWYER: And to my second son, Frank, the same. The two new estates to be maintained and run completely independently.

WILLIAM: He promised it to me, all of it. This is your doing.

FRANK: Me? Since when could I change the old man's mind about anything?

LAWYER: The division to be made according to the attached map.

WILLIAM: Give me that.

FRANK: Don't be such a bad loser, Will. The old man always said he'd treat us equally.

WILLIAM: Ha, ha, ha.

FRANK: What's so funny?

WILLIAM: Everything. Pa's idea of equality wasn't exactly the same as yours.

FRANK: Show me. No! Can he do this? Well?

LAWYER: Is there some difficulty?

WILLIAM: None in the world. I get all the good farmland. Brother Frank gets the marsh and the scrubs. No difficulty there.

FRANK: Damn the man. Damn you too. Well, let's see if you're smiling this time next year.

WILLIAM: What do you mean?

FRANK: Let's see how your precious farmlands cope when they're next door to my mines and my machinery.

WILLIAM: You're going to mine the land?

FRANK: Those coalseams are worth ten times your wheatfields, brother.

WILLIAM: You can't do it.

FRANK: You can't stop me.

LAWYER: Yes, he can.

FRANK: What?

SOLICITOR: Yes, he can.

WILLIAM: I thought you'd finished. Yes. How can I stop him?

FRANK: Yes, how?

LAWYER: This is your late's father's final stipulation. Neither of you may do anything to exploit his share of the lands either for minerals or development without the full and complete consent of the other. He can stop you with a single word.

WILLIAM: No!

MADELEINE: That was in 1882. Or was it 3? 3, I'm sure.

WILLIAM: No!

MADELEINE: Father!

WILLIAM: I can still see his face.

MADELEINE: After nearly forty years?

WILLIAM: It could be a hundred. It wouldn't make any difference.

MADELEINE: Father, why did you hate him so much? He was your brother!

WILLIAM: Half-brother.

MADELEINE: And that's a reason? He had such a terrible life.

VICAR: In the sure and certain hope of the resurrection to eternal life still to come. Amen.

CONGREGATION: Amen.

WILLIAM: No.

FRANK JUN: Uncle William.

WILLIAM: Have you inherited your father's stupidity, sir? No, never, not while I'm alive.

MADELEINE: Frank was lying just inside the door. Daddy, my father, was slumped across his desk. The gun was at his feet. His head was …

MAX CARRADOS: I understand.

MADELEINE: I'm so sorry.

MAX CARRADOS: Why are you carrying a newspaper, Miss Whitmarsh?

MADELEINE: What? I'm sorry?

MAX CARRADOS: Two things were immediately apparent as you walked into this room. You're dressed in mourning and you're carrying a newspaper. I assume that it has something to do with this business.

MADELEINE: Yes, yes, it does.

MAX CARRADOS: May I have it, please?

MADELEINE: But surely?

MAX CARRADOS: If you please.

MADELEINE: Of course. Here.

MAX CARRADOS: Thank you. Ah, this is not a national. The grade of paper.

MADELEINE: It's the Sli…

MAX CARRADOS: Slimbridge Herald.

MADELEINE: Mr Carrados!

MAX CARRADOS: Banner headlines are always slightly raised from the page. It's no great feat to feel the letters with one's fingers. Ah, so it's front page news. Mysterious Tragedy at Tillingshaw.

MADELEINE: That's amazing.

MAX CARRADOS: By no means. Beyond the headline things do become rather trickier. Suicide follows attempted murder. Attempted murder, Miss Whitmarsh?

MADELEINE: Yes, I was, I was just about to tell you.

SERVANT: God save us. God save us.

SERVANT: God have mercy. He's alive.

FRANK JUN: Yes.

SERVANT: Easy, sir. Don't try to move.

FRANK JUN: No, I'm all right.

SERVANT: All right? Look, there's no blood. Your father must have missed him.

FRANK JUN: No, no, I felt the shot.

SERVANT: Then how in the world?

FRANK JUN: I don't know. Lord, surely not. Help me to sit up.

SERVANT: Here you are, sir.

FRANK JUN: Now, let's see.

SERVANT: What's happened to your watch. Mind the glass, sir.

FRANK JUN: I just want to see if I can open it. Yes. Will you take a look at that?

SERVANT: Heaven defend us. It's a miracle.

FRANK JUN: Good old watch, eh? Who'd have thought it?

MADELEINE: The bullet was inside the works. The back was all dented but it hadn't gone right through.

MAX CARRADOS: A miracle indeed. Not exactly in my line, you know, investigating miracles.

Unit 17 Listening Exercise 1

Answers
– There are footprints in the butter.
– A newspaper.

Unit 20 Listening Exercise 2

It is spring and all along our street the teenagers are running amok. In the light evenings and through the open windows they can be seen and heard shrieking, skulking, turning to sex, drugs, 18-plus videos and undesirable friends, kicking footballs about and setting off the fire alarms. An upmarket brand of youth can sometimes be seen lolling against the front garden walls, employing a cordless telephone.

In our house the telephone rings relentlessly. Treasure's life has opened out on the end of it. She can Go Out with people by telephone and she can Dump Them. She can have whole relationships without any physical contact. Once on it she loses track of time, even peak time. It flies by at 38p a minute.

I've tried limiting her telephoning – between 8 and 9 was to be Treasure's phoning time, otherwise – and this is the ultimate threat – I will be rude to them.

'I hate you,' shrieks the Treasure. 'Nobody else's mother is so nasty and spiteful.' She is already deeply ashamed of me. 'Everybody knows I've got a mother with red glasses who swears,' she weeps. 'I hate you.'

She hasn't quite understood my instructions, assuming not that she *may* use the phone between eight and nine, but that she *must*. On the dot of eight, she springs to it and phones like billy-oh. Eager for calls she snatches up the receiver, mid first ring. Should I use the phone even briefly during *her* time, say to ask my neighbour for a carrot, Treasure is incensed. 'This is MY time!' she bellows.

'All girls are like this,' says my neighbour, Mrs Perez. Hers are now twenty and twenty-one and living elsewhere. Boys are apparently different, more curt. I spoke to one this afternoon by telephone while the house was empty.

'Is your mother in?'
'No'
'Could you please tell her I phoned?'
'Erp.'
'Goodbye.'
'Erp.'

I never wanted a son before.

Phonetic symbols

LONG VOWELS

iː sheep /ʃiːp/	ɑː farm /£fɑːm/ /$fɑːrm/	ɔː horse /£hɔːs/ /$hɔːrs/	uː shoe /ʃuː/	ɜː bird /£bɜːd/ /$bɜːrd/

SHORT VOWELS

ɪ ship /ʃɪp/	e head /hed/	æ hat /hæt/	ʌ cup /kʌp/	(Br)ɒ sock /£sɒk/	ʊ foot /fʊt/	ə above /əˈbʌv/	(Am)ɚ mother /$ˈmʌð·ɚ/

DIPHTHONGS (Two vowel sounds together)

eɪ day /deɪ/	aɪ eye /aɪ/	ɔɪ boy /bɔɪ/	aʊ mouth /maʊθ/	(Br)əʊ nose /£nəʊz/	(Am)oʊ nose /$noʊz/	(Br)ɪə ear /£ɪəʳ/	(Br)ea hair /£heaʳ/	(Br)ʊə pure /£pjʊəʳ/

CONSONANTS

voiceless	p pen /pen/	t town /taʊn/	k cat /kæt/	f fish /fɪʃ/	θ think /θɪŋk/	s say /seɪ/	ʃ she /ʃiː/	tʃ cheese /tʃiːz/
voiced	b book /bʊk/	d day /deɪ/	g give /gɪv/	v very /ˈver·ɪ/	ð the /ðə/	z zoo /zuː/	ʒ vision /vɪʒn/	dʒ jump /dʒʌmp/
	l look /lʊk/	r run /rʌn/	j yes /jes/	w we /wiː/	m moon /muːn/	n name /neɪm/	ŋ sing /sɪŋ/	h hand /hænd/

Acknowledgements

The author would like to thank the following people: editors Helena Gomm, Barbara Thomas, Liz Sharman and Lindsay White; designers Nick Newton and Randell Harris; everybody at Cambridge University Press for making this book possible.

The author and publishers would like to thank the teachers and students who trialled and commented on the material and whose feedback was invaluable.

The author and publishers are grateful to the authors, publishers and others who have given permission for the use of copyright material identified in the text. It has not been possible to identify the sources of all the material used and in such cases the publishers would welcome information from copyright owners. Apologies are expressed for any omissions.

The BBC World Service for Listening Exercise 1 on p. 7 in the Student's Book and cassette from the programme *Outlook*; *The Observer* for Exercise 3 on p. 9 and Exercise 1 on pp. 10 and 11; Cambridge University Press for the texts on pp. 13 and 74 from *David Crystal, Cambridge Encyclopedia of the English Language*, for the dictionary entries on p. 17 and p. 34 from the *Cambridge International Dictionary of English*, for the extracts on pp. 128, 129 and 130 from *The History and Social Influence of the Potato* by Redcliffe Salaman and for the book covers on p. 132: *The Ecology of Preschool Behaviour* by Peter K. Smith and Kevin J, Connolly, *The Early History of the Viol* by Ian Woodfield, *The Transformation of German Academic Medicine, 1750-1820* by Thomas H. Broman and *The Roman Law Tradition* edited by A. D. E. Lewis D. J. Ibbetson; Celtic Music for the song on p. 21 by Dick Gaughan; John Murray and Desmond Elliott for the poem 'Harrow-on-the-Hill' on p. 22 by John Betjeman; John Robb for the article and Make-up for the photograph on p. 23; *The Times* for the texts on pp. 28, 50-51, 99 and 100-102 © Times Newspapers Limited, (1994, 1995); *The Sun* for the text on p. 31; The BBC, the late Kenneth Williams, Derek Nimmo and Peter Jones for Listening Exercise 2 on p. 34 extract from 'Just a Minute'; HarperCollins Publishers, Jed Mattes Inc. and Greene and Heaton Ltd for Listening Exercise 1 on p. 49, © 1991 by Bill Bryson published by Secker & Warburg. Reproduced by permission of Greene & Heaton Ltd; Little, Brown and Company Publishers and Curtis Brown Ltd for the poem in Listening Exercise 1 on p. 55–56 from *Verses from 1929 on* by Ogden Nash. Copyright 1947 by Ogden Nash. First appeared in *The New Yorker*. Reprinted by permission of Little, Brown and Company and Curtis Brown, Ltd. Copyright © 1949 by Ogden Nash, renewed; Papermac and Curtis Brown Agents for the poem on p. 58 by Thomas Hardy from *Selected Shorter Poems of Thomas Hardy* . Reproduced by kind permission of the Estate of Thomas Hardy, © the Estate of Thomas Hardy; Silva Screen Records, Chappell Music, IMP and Hal Leonard for the song by Lesley Garrett in Exercise 4 on p. 59; Peters Fraser & Dunlop for the poem in Writing Exercise 2 on p. 60 extract from *Pie in the Sky* by Roger McGough. Reprinted by permission of The Peters Fraser & Dunlop Group Limited on behalf of Roger McGough; The BBC, Peter Hobday and Abby Redhead for the extract from 'The Today Programme' in Listening Exercises 1, 2 and 3 on p. 63; *Private Eye* for text i on p. 64; Artellus Ltd for the story in Unit 10 pp. 68-73 *The Perfect Pair* by Nicholas Coleridge; The BBC for the extract in the Listening exercise on p. 77 from a speech by Jo Grimond; Marks & Spencer for the texts on p. 83; *The Financial Times* for the text on p. 87, © *The Financial Times* 1994; Professor Susan Greenfield for the speech in Listening Exercise 1 on p. 89 extract from a Royal Society Christmas Lecture, 1994; AND Reference Data for the illustrations no b on pp. 95, 96 and 97, © AND Reference Data, Oxford, UK; Mr Punch Productions and MBA Literary Agents for the extract in Unit 15 p. 108–113 from the radio drama *The Eyes of Max Carrados* by Ernest Bramah, adapted by Bert Coules; Ewan MacNaughton Associates for the article on p. 115 (top) from *The Daily Telegraph*, © Telegraph Group Limited, London, 1994; *The Daily Star* for the article on p. 115 (bottom), © Express Newspapers, 1994; Piaktus Books for the text on p. 118 extract from *All In A Day's Work* edited by Mark Hornsby; *The Guardian* for the article on p. 119, © *The Guardian*, 1994; Motivation

Cassettes Ltd for the extract in the Listening exercise on p. 137 from *Sales Boosters no 10: Negotiations Techniques for the New Salesman*; HarperCollins Publishers for the extract on p. 139 from *Beware Those Who Ask for Feedback* by Richard A. Moran; *The Economist* for the article on p. 142, © *The Economist*, London, 1996; Little Brown, The Judy Martin Agency and Palmer and Dodge for the extracts on p. 144 and 145 and in the Listening exercise on p. 147 from *Treasure: The Trials of a Teenage Terror* by Gina Davidson; Sheil Land Associates for the back cover blurb on p. 151 and the extract A on p. 154 from *A Suitable Boy* by Vikram Seth; Michael O'Mara Books Ltd for the back cover blurb on p. 151 and the extracts on B on p. 153 and p.154 from *Ghosts for Christmas: Wolverden Tower* and *The Snow* by Hugh Walpole, edited by Richard Dalby; The Orion Publishing Group for the back cover blurb on p. 152 and the extract on p. 155 from *The Glass Lake* by Maeve Binchy; Penguin UK and Aitken & Stone for the back cover blurb on p. 152 and the extract D p. 155 from *The London Embassy* by Paul Theroux, © Paul Theroux, 1982; Harlequin, Mills and Boon Ltd for the extract in the Listening exercise p. 154 from *'And he kissed her' A Guide to Writing Romantic Fiction* cassette, reprinted and recorded with the permission of Harlequin, Mills & Boon Limited; The extract in the Listening exercise p. 158 is from *Sporting Gaffes* , reproduced courtesy of the BBC; Apple Computer Inc. for the extract F on p. 160 from the *Macintosh Performa User's Guide 1995*, © Apple Computer, Inc. 1995. Used with permission. All rights reserved; Jean Aitchison for the extract in the Listening exercise 3 p. 161 from the fourth Reith Lecture, February 1996.

The appearance of logos and trademarks in this book in no way affects their legal status as trademarks.

The publishers and author are grateful to the following illustrators and photographic sources:

Illustrators: Abbas: p. 89; Rowan Barnes-Murphy: pp. 57, 125; Chris Burke: pp. 34, 45, 91, 123, 159; Philip Emms: pp. 18, 63 *b*, 119, 121; Annie Farrall: pp. 44, 68, 70, 71, 72, 145, 147; Martin Fish: pp. 29, 116, 144; Mark McLaughlin: pp. 43, 56, 113, 153; Diane Oliver: pp. 14, 66, 106; Tracy Rich: pp. 12, 16, 19, 39 *t*, 63 *t*, 80, 84, 95, 96, 97, 108, 109, 129; Sam Thompson: pp. 58, 60, 101, 104, 156; Katherine Walker: pp. 54, 73, 79; Bob Wilson: pp. 39 *b*, 64, 65, 94, 137, 164; Annabel Wright: pp. 22, 37, 55, 110, 127, 131, 140.

Photographic sources: Art Directors and TRIP Photo Library: pp. 49 *tl*, 76 *b*, 143 *bl*; The Aviation Picture Library: p. 87 *t, b*; BBC Picture Archives: p. 31 *t*; The Bridgeman Art Library Ltd: p. 58; Civic Centre Library, London Borough of Harrow: p. 22; Collections: pp. 20, 76 *t*; E R Degginger/Science Photo Library: p. 63; Simon Fraser/Science Photo Library: p. 89 *tr*; The Ronald Grant Archive: p. 98 *br*; Sally and Richard Greenhill: pp. 91, 114 *ml*, 143 *bcr*, 157 *mt*, 157 *mb*, 157 *bl*, 157 *br*; The Hulton Getty Picture Collection Ltd: pp. 77, 130; The Image Bank: pp. 49 *br*, 53 *tr*, 114 *bl*, 143 *bcc*, 143 *bcl*; The Kobal Collection: pp. 9 *bl, bc*, 98 *t, bl*; Pictor International Ltd: pp. 53 *tl*, 82 *t, b*, 93 *t*, 114 *mc*; 136 *b*, 143 *tl, tc*; PolyGram/Pictorial Press Ltd: p. 53 *b*; Popperfoto: p. 76 *ml*; PowerStock Ltd: pp. 31 *m*, 40 *bc, r*, 114 *tr*, 136 *ml*; Ernest Proctor/Bridgeman Art Library: p. 61; Rosenfield Images Ltd/Science Photo Library: p. 35; Science Photo Library: p. 7 *m*; Scottish National Portrait Gallery/The Bridgeman Art Library Ltd: p.19; Blair Seitz/Science Photo Library: p. 40 *tc*; Frank Spooner Pictures Ltd: pp. 9 *br*, 10, 31 *b*; Tony Stone Images: pp. 6, 40 *tl, bl*, 49 *bl*, *tc, tr*, 62, 93 *b*, 114 *mr*, 136 *tr, mr*, 139, 143 *tr*, 157 *tl*, 157 *tr*; Southern Studios: p. 23; Telegraph Colour Library: p. 143 *br*; Geoff Tompkinson/Science Photo Library: p. 89 *tl*; Topham Picturepoint: pp. 7 *t*, 76 *mr*; The Visual Arts Library London: p. 127; Woodfall Wild Images: p. 36.

Commissioned photography: Jeremy Pembrey: pp.27, 43 *t*, 43 *b*, 51, 103, 149.

t = top, *m*= middle, *b* = bottom, *l* = left, *c* = centre, *r* = right

Picture research by Mandy Twells

Design and composition by Newton Harris